SLOW COOKER
CENTRAL

KIDS

SLOW COOKER CENTRAL

KIDS

Paulene Christie

ABC Books

The ABC 'Wave' device is a trademark of the Australian Broadcasting Corporation and is used under licence by HarperCollinsPublishers Australia.

First published in Australia in 2018
by HarperCollins*Publishers* Australia Pty Limited
ABN 36 009 913 517
harpercollins.com.au

Introduction copyright © Paulene Christie 2018
Compilation copyright © HarperCollins*Publishers* Australia Pty Limited 2018
Copyright in the contributor recipes remains the property of the individual contributors.

The right of Paulene Christie to be identified as the author of this work has been asserted by her in accordance with the *Copyright Amendment (Moral Rights) Act 2000*. This work is copyright. Apart from any use as permitted under the Copyright Act 1968, no part may be reproduced, copied, scanned, stored in a retrieval system, recorded, or transmitted, in any form or by any means, without the prior written permission of the publisher.

HarperCollins*Publishers*
Level 13, 201 Elizabeth Street, Sydney NSW 2000, Australia
Unit D1, 63 Apollo Drive, Rosedale, Auckland 0632, New Zealand
A 53, Sector 57, Noida, UP, India
1 London Bridge Street, London SE1 9GF, United Kingdom
2 Bloor Street East, 20th floor, Toronto, Ontario M4W 1A8, Canada
195 Broadway, New York NY 10007, USA

A catalogue record for this book is available from the National Library of Australia

ISBN: 978 0 7333 3922 6 (paperback)
ISBN: 978 1 4607 0958 0 (ebook)

Cover design by HarperCollins Design Studio
Cover images by Shutterstock
Internal design by HarperCollins Design Studio
Author photograph by Tina Baills
Typeset in Adobe Jenson by Kirby Jones
Printed and bound in Australia by McPhersons Printing Group
The papers used by HarperCollins in the manufacture of this book are a natural, recyclable product made from wood grown in sustainable plantation forests. The fibre source and manufacturing processes meet recognized international environmental standards, and carry certification.

*Dedicated to my groom & and our miracles
Simon, Caleb, Talyn and Ella
xx My world xx*

Contents

Introduction	1
Slow Cooking for Kids	3
Slow Cooker Hints & Tips	7
Baby & Toddler	31
Breakfast	39
Super Sides	49
Snacks & Lunchbox	63
Fussy Eaters	77
Slow Cooker in a Hurry	91
Everyday Crowdpleasers	109
Home Takeaway	135
Winter Warmers	145
Dinner Hits	161
Mince & Meatballs	195
Birthday Party	213
A Little Bit Fancy	225
Sweet Treats	247
Projects	261
Index	268
Acknowledgements	279

INTRODUCTION

Welcome to book four in the Slow Cooker Central series!

These books are founded on the recipes created, shared and inspired by our Facebook group 'Slow Cooker Recipes 4 Families' and from our 'Slow Cooker Central' website community.

Founded in 2012, we are a passionate community of men, women and young people from all over the world, sharing a love and enjoyment of slow cooking and the creative, tasty, budget and family friendly meals we can easily cook in our slow cookers.

In our first two books, *Slow Cooker Central* in 2015 and *Slow Cooker Central 2* in 2016, we gave you hundreds of varied and delicious recipes to cook in your slow cooker.

For book three in 2017, you told us you needed great family recipes that were focused on being inexpensive and easy for anyone on a budget to enjoy. Boy, did we deliver just that with *Slow Cooker Central Super Savers*!

All three books rocketed to the top of the Australian bestseller charts so we know you loved them just as much as we did!

I'm eternally blessed to know that our books sit on bookshelves all over the world and I'm always humbled by the passion our readers have for our books, how much they love them and love all the recipes they cook from them.

This time around you told us you'd love a book with a KIDS focus. Easy recipes that kids will eat without complaint and perhaps even help you cook. Well get ready kids, because here it is!

If you like recipes with simple ingredients, simple methods, tried and tested tasty outcomes – that's what we have for you. Get those kids involved in cooking with you, or get them licking their plates clean without complaint ... just get them into these recipes and you'll be so happy you did!

As a busy mum of three I know what a stressful time dinner time can be with fussy eaters and I'm here to help. I've tested all my recipes on my own children, and all those who entered their recipes into this book did the same. We are confident the little people in your life will enjoy the ideas in the pages to follow.

There's nothing overly difficult to prepare, or too spicy to enjoy, or too complex to cook – just great-tasting recipes that everyday people can cook and trust that they'll have a fantastic outcome every time. Of course, these aren't recipes only for children. Anyone can enjoy the great recipes in these pages no matter what their age.

At Slow Cooker Central our motto has always been 'Real food, cooked by real people, in real kitchens!'.

No overly styled glossy studio food photos that no one can ever feel they could succeed in replicating when they cook at home.

No expensive, exotic ingredients that most don't have on hand or can't afford to buy simply for one recipe.

No overly complicated methods that you need a chef's training and a tool shed of gadgets to complete.

REAL food. REAL results. REALLY good taste.

So, when you get home with this book, sit down somewhere comfortable and have a stack of post-it notes at the ready. Because we are confident that you'll find PLENTY of recipes among these pages that you will want to try! The hardest decision you'll have to make is which one to cook first :)

Happy slow cooking everyone. xx

Paulene Christie

SLOW COOKER
CENTRAL

KIDS

Is there anything more frustrating for a parent than that screwed up little face of a young one pushing their plate away uneaten at the dinner table and declaring, 'I don't like it!!'?

Aaaargh!!!

Often you have spent all day shopping, preparing and cooking that meal. Feeling sure you'll strike parental gold and have a meal everyone at the table eats without complaint. A meal they'll all finish enthusiastically and say 'That was great mum, can we have that one more often?'

We wish, right!

How great would it be to have meals that you can serve *knowing* they will be a hit with your littlest critics, but that don't only consist of chicken nuggets, pizza or hot chips smothered in sauce.

In *Slow Cooker Central Kids* we want to give you options that are popular, that are tasty, and that can still be nutritious!

A great way to get kids enthused about eating a meal is to give them ownership of its creation. Why not let your kids look through these pages with you? Have them pick out some meals they think they'll like. Then plan a shopping list and a little trip to the supermarket with them for anything you need, then get them in the kitchen cooking with you! It's fun for them to be involved (even though, let's face it, it's sometime a little messier, ha-ha).

It's also a great skill that you can give them. Have them grow up knowing they have what it takes to put a great meal on the table. You'll build not only their skills, but also their self confidence! Instil a love of cooking in them early on and you'll equip them with something they will use for the rest of their life.

And, fingers crossed, as they get a little older but are still living at home, they may just take over cooking the odd family meal for you every now and then (hoorah!).

A big advantage of slow cooking is that it's much safer for little people to be involved in than other methods. No saucepans of boiling water, hot spitting fat in fry pans, no scorching hot ovens to contend with.

If any such steps are required to prep any ingredients for our recipes, they are minimal, and you can help with that or anything needing knives and other sharps first, then hand things over to junior (under your supervision) to do the rest.

Maybe they'll need an apron and a kitchen stool to feel extra special and able to help you get your cook on. Just be sure to help them wash those little hands well first. ;)

Cooking is also a great way for kids to form a healthy relationship with food for later life. They'll know more about how it's prepared, what it costs, and how to take simple, healthy ingredients and combine them to get the tastes they love.

It's great for their motor skills and co-ordination as they wash, peel, cut and prep.

It's great for reading and comprehension skills as they work through step by step instructions.

It's great quality time for you and your kids to spend together, working in the kitchen on a shared project.

It's also a great opportunity to pass on your own kitchen skills to them and to teach them family recipes handed down through the generations.

There are so many reasons to get our kids cooking and no reasons not to! So why not give it a go!

The recipes in *Slow Cooker Central Kids* are easy enough for you to cook with or for them, but most importantly are tasty enough to still be enjoyed by the whole family. So even if they don't want to cook them with you, they can enjoy eating them with you.

And we've even included some fancier dishes for special occasions and party food for celebrations too to cater to all ages and skills!

So let's get started!

SLOW COOKER HINTS & TIPS

We have here what we hope is a great collection of tips and tricks and frequently asked questions that we have gathered from the collective experience in our slow cooking community.

We've covered some really important safety do's and don'ts to help you to get the very best out of your slow cooking experiments while minimising the risks that other cooks may unknowingly take. The section on the tea-towel trick helps explain what that strategy is all about – you will see it mentioned a lot in our recipes. It helps us make many of the unique and unusual dishes we create in our slow cookers.

So BEFORE you start cooking, have a read through the hints and tips that follow – and then your hardest decision after that will only be deciding which great recipe from the book to cook first.

Can I use frozen meat in the slow cooker?

This is a hotly debated topic. The short answer is yes, you *could*, but no – you should not! Many people will tell you they have done so for years and it's never hurt them. However, that's probably more to do with luck than anything else. Don't follow dangerous advice. It's a risk that is quite frankly unnecessary, and we hope is one that you won't take with yourself or those being served your meals. Here's why…

Health concerns

Although some people will state that they cook frozen meat in their slow cookers, the health and food technology experts say that for food safety reasons you should bring your food to temperatures of 60°C (140°F) or more as quickly as possible. Some people assume that cooking frozen meat in a slow cooker works the same way as with other methods, but they are not the same. Food cooked in the oven or on a stovetop heats up much faster than in a slow cooker. Cooking frozen meat in a slow cooker significantly increases the amount of time it takes for food to reach the safe temperature target, and thus significantly increases the chances of you and your family getting food poisoning.

Cooker care

Cooking meat from frozen also increases the risk of a ceramic slow cooker bowl cracking as a result of the wide difference in temperature between the frozen food and the heating bowl. If the bowl cracks, your slow cooker is unusable.

On a similar note, you should always remove the food from your slow cooker dish before refrigerating it. The nature of the thick ceramic bowl means it retains heat and thus takes a lot longer to cool down to safe refrigeration temperatures, once again leaving your food too long in the danger zone.

In Summary

Please don't prioritise convenience over safety. It may be that you have to take the time to defrost your meat first, or you may in fact have to change the meal you had planned to cook for today until tomorrow when you can have the meat defrosted – but it's worth it. I for one will not take that risk with my loved ones. You are free to weigh up this risk for you and your family and hopefully make the safe decision for your home. Cook smart – cook safe.

How can I thicken slow-cooker recipes with a high liquid content?

Slow cooking can produce dishes with excess liquid due to condensation forming on the lid and the fact the lid stays closed so the liquid doesn't reduce as with some stovetop or oven methods. Here's a collection of tips and trick you can use to ensure a thickened consistency to your final dish.

Cornflour (cornstarch)

Mix 1–2 tablespoons of cornflour with 1–2 tablespoons of cool tap water and mix until it becomes a thin runny paste without any lumps (some people prefer to use rice flour or arrowroot flour). Pour this mix straight into your slow cooker dish 20–30 minutes before serving and stir briefly around whatever is in the pot. Then leave the dish to continue cooking, preferably on HIGH but LOW if the recipe requires.

This added cornflour will thicken the liquids in the recipe. If this amount of cornflour doesn't thicken the liquids sufficiently, you can repeat the process. But take care not to add too much cornflour to your recipe – one or two additions are usually all that's needed. Some people ladle the liquid out of the slow cooker into a saucepan on the stove and add the cornflour there. How you do it is totally up to you.

Gravy granules/powder
Substitute gravy granules for cornflour and follow the method as described above. The suitability of this option will depend on the recipe and whether the addition of gravy will suit it.

Grated potato
Grate 1–2 raw potatoes and add them to the slow cooker 30–45 minutes before serving. Stir them as much as you can around the solid ingredients. This will very quickly thicken the dish and the remaining cooking time will allow the potato to cook through.

Grated potato will only suit some recipes – those with vegetable or potato already in them or which would be complemented by the addition of potato.

You can use instant potato flakes in place of grated raw potato.

Lift the lid
Another option is to remove the lid of the slow cooker or at least place it ajar for the last 30 minutes of cooking to enable the sauce to thicken through evaporation. This is not ideal as the very nature of the slow cooker is to provide a sealed environment to maintain the cooking temperature – but it is an option.

Use less liquid to begin with
A natural consequence of slow cooking is the increased moisture content thanks to the drip condensation from the lid down into the food during cooking. Many people think meat has to be covered in liquid to slow cook it, but in fact it needs very little liquid. If you find a dish is regularly ending up with far too much liquid, reduce the liquid in the initial recipe next time you cook it.

The tea towel trick
While the tea towel trick (see the next page) is normally used when slow cooking cakes and breads, it can be used to absorb some of the condensation from the dish when following non-baking recipes. Please read important safety information in the section regarding the tea towel trick.

Flour toss

Tossing your meat in flour before cooking can also thicken the dish.

Pulling/shredding

Pulling or shredding your meat at the end of the cooking time (assuming this suits the dish) will also take up a lot of the excess liquids in the pot.

The tea towel (dish towel) trick

Quite a few of the recipes in this book will ask you to 'Cook with a tea towel (dish towel) under the lid'. The tea towel, which lies between the top of the slow cooker bowl and the lid of the slow cooker, acts to absorb condensation and stop it from dripping down into the food cooking inside. It's often used when you wouldn't want the cake or bread being cooked ending up soggy.

Note that this method has been devised by home slow cooker enthusiasts and is not recommended officially or declared a safe practice by slow cooker manufacturers. Please carefully read the following information before deciding for yourself if it's something you wish to do.

When using the tea towel trick, regular users suggest you fold up any excess fabric from the towel up onto the lid of the slow cooker, securing it to the lid handle, so it doesn't hang down over the hot outer casing of the slow cooker – this is very important for safety! A tea towel on the lid absorbs liquid during the cooking process, so it stays somewhat damp and is unlikely to burn.

If you have concerns about the fire hazards related to this practice, you can research the safety issues involved and inform yourself about the pros and cons. It is totally up to you to appraise the risks and decide whether it is safe to use the tea towel method with your slow cooker.

It is not recommended to use the tea towel in general slow cooking, but just as an optional measure to reduce liquid in a dish. If you decide to use this technique, do so only for cakes, breads and baking or recipes where water dripping is a major issue.

Please make your own decision regarding the safety of this practice. If in any doubt, do not do this. I personally recommend you don't leave your home when you are using a tea towel in this way, so that you are able to keep an eye on your slow cooker and the towel.

How can I remove oil and fat from a slow cooker dish?

There are several methods you can use to remove oil from your dish. First and foremost, you can reduce the amount of fat going into the dish at the beginning.

Be choosy
Choose lean cuts of meat, trim visible fat from meat and add little to no oil to your slow cooker recipes.

Prep it
Pre-browning or sealing meat in a frying pan is one way to remove some of the fat before cooking it in the slow cooker (read more about pre-browning and sealing meat on page 15).

Skim and discard
Perhaps the most obvious solution is to spoon that fat right out of there! Towards the end of the cooking process, the fat will often gather at the top of your dish so you can use a ladle or spoon to gently remove and discard it.

The ice-cube trick
Placing ice-cubes briefly on top of the dish will cause the fat to 'stick to' the ice-cubes (because the lower temperature causes the fat to solidify). You can then discard the ice-cubes and the oil right along with them.

The bread trick
Very briefly lay a piece of bread along the top of the dish. This will soak up the fat, which can be discarded with the bread or fed to a four-legged friend. But be very careful and always remove the bread with tongs, as it will be hot!

Some people use paper towel instead of bread to soak up the fats and oils, but if something is going to break down in my food, I would rather it were bread than paper.

Cool and skim
If you have the time or you are cooking a recipe in advance, you can cool the entire dish in the fridge overnight. The fat will solidify on top and you can remove it before reheating and serving the dish.

What does the AUTO function on my slow cooker do?

Many slow cookers have LOW, HIGH, KEEP WARM and AUTO settings. The AUTO function usually means the dish will begin cooking at HIGH for approximately 2 hours, then the slow cooker will switch itself down to the LOW temperature setting. (The dial itself doesn't move and will remain pointing to AUTO.)

This feature varies with different slow cooker models and brands, so always consult your user manual.

Are timers safe to use for slow cooking?

There is an important distinction between timers built in to a slow cooker and the wall kind that you plug into the power socket and then plug your slow cooker into.

A slow cooker with a timer function will generally switch your unit to a 'keep warm' mode after your pre-selected cooking time is complete. Most units will then only stay in this keep-warm mode for a limited number of hours for food safety reasons.

Wall timers are not recommended for slow cooking. For good reasons:

- Some people use them to delay the start time of cooking. This means the ingredients are sitting out, not cooking, for several hours before the slow cooker turns on. It's a recipe for a food-poisoning disaster.
- Some people use them to turn off the slow cooker at the end of the cooking time completely. This means your finished hot – and slowly getting cooler – dish is sitting out multiplying nasty bacteria in it until you get around to eating it. Again a recipe for a food-poisoning disaster. You would not cook a meal in your oven then just leave it in there or sitting on the kitchen bench for hours before eating it. A slow cooked meal is no different.

Definitely avoid timers designed for light fittings. These timers are not made to handle the load of a slow cooker. It could cause the slow cooker to burn out the element, or the timer itself could burn out or catch fire.

Cook smart, cook safe – please do not use wall timers for slow cooking.

Is it safe to leave my slow cooker unattended all day while I am out of the house?

In short, yes ... with precautions.

Slow cookers are designed to run all day unattended without posing a fire hazard. There are, however, further precautions you can take if you're concerned.

- I always place my slow cookers on top of my ceramic cooktop. This surface is designed to withstand high temperatures, after all. Just be sure never to accidentally have a hotplate turned on (I lost my first ever slow cooker to this happening when I melted its legs off!). If you don't have this option, placing the cooker on a glass-top trivet or heavy cutting board works in a similar way.
- Ensure flammable objects are not left touching or anywhere near the slow cooker.
- Move the slow cooker away from the wall and any curtains, etc.
- Do not use the tea towel method if you are out of the house.
- Always have a working smoke alarm and electrical safety switch in your home so that if you are home and the worst somehow happens, you and your family will be alerted to the danger and the electricity supply will shut off.

Is it okay to open the lid of my slow cooker to stir my dish or check on it?

Many of us have heard the tale that each time you open the lid of your slow cooker, it adds 30 minutes to the cooking time.

In practice, I have never personally found this to be true. If I am at home I am a habitual lid-lifter, often pausing to look at, stir, taste or even smell my dish throughout the day. And if anything, my dishes often cook much faster than I might expect.

However, slow cookers rely on the slow build-up of heat to cook food to perfection. Lifting the lid during cooking lets built-up heat escape and will lower the temperature in the slow cooker. Stirring the contents allows even more heat to escape from the lower layers of the food. Once the lid is replaced, it will take an amount of time for the food to heat back up to its previous temperature.

So the choice is up to you. Resist if you can, or don't. You will soon come to know your own slow cooker (or if you are like me and have several, you will get to know each of their little quirks and cooking times and temps).

Do I need to pre-brown, pre-cook or seal my meat before placing it in the slow cooker?

This is a debate that has no right or wrong answer. Some people are fierce advocates of browning meat prior to slow cooking it ... while just as many are fiercely against doing so.

At the end of the day it comes down to your own personal choice.

But let's look at the reasons on both sides of the debate so you can decide what YOU want to do.

Reasons to brown
- Faster cooking time – meat that is pre-browned won't need as much cooking time.
- Lock in moisture – sealing the surface of the meat can seal in extra moisture.
- Increased flavour – those caramelised, brown yummy bits on the surface of your meat that come with browning have lots of flavour that would otherwise be missing from your finished dish. Browning with herbs or spices can also increase the richness of these flavours in your recipe.
- Appearance – sometimes despite no change in taste, browned meat benefits the presentation of the final dish. By contrast, meat juices released from unsealed meat can sometimes mix with sauces etc making it appear as if cream-based sauces have split, when they have not.
- Fat removal – browning meat before cooking and then discarding the liquids produced is a great way to eliminate some of the fat from your finished dish. This is especially true when browning mince or ground beef.
- Thickening – meat dredged in flour, then browned before slow cooking, will add to the thickness of the sauce in the final dish.

Reasons not to brown
- Convenience – this would have to be the number one reason. Many of us are drawn to slow cooking by the sheer convenience of pouring

a collection of ingredients into the bowl, turning on the machine and walking away. This convenience is lessened when you have to add extra steps to pre-brown.
- Time factor – pre-browning meat tends to reduce the cooking time for the recipe. This works against many slow cookers who rely on the extended slow cooking period to make it work for them, for example when they work all day.
- Less mess – while many new slow cookers allow the option to sear in the same bowl as you slow cook, this is not possible with the traditional ceramic bowl slow cookers. Thus browning a dish means dirtying a frying pan. Let's face it, who likes extra dishes? Not me!
- No option – we see many of our members using slow cookers when they don't have access to stoves/ovens. In this instance they do not have the option to brown their meats but shouldn't think that means they can't slow cook a dish that asks for it.

In summary
It really is up to you.

Personally I very rarely brown – maybe 5 per cent of the time that I slow cook, and then it's almost only those recipes which call for thin strips of meat to be flour coated and browned prior to slow cooking.

Some days and with some recipes you will want to – others you'll want to just dump in your ingredients, set and forget. Neither way is right or wrong, but hopefully in these pages we have given you the information to decide what's right for you.

Can I slow cook a whole chicken?

You sure can! And many people will tell you that having tried slow cooking chickens whole they will never cook them any other way.

Here are some tips to keep in mind.

- You don't need to add any liquids to the slow cooker with your chicken. You will be really surprised by just how much liquid a whole chicken will release during cooking! And because a slow cooker is sealed, that liquid won't evaporate.

- Cook your chicken with the breast-side down. This keeps the breast meat sitting in the liquid that's produced during cooking so it won't dry out.
- If you are concerned there is too much liquid, or if you have a spice rub etc on your chicken that you don't want to get too immersed in liquid, you may choose to elevate the chicken above the bottom of your slow cooker by sitting it on some scrunched up aluminium foil balls, egg rings or even an inverted dish.
- When it comes to seasoning your chicken, your imagination is your only limit. Whatever spice, marinade or herbs you may use when you cook a chicken in the oven you can use just as well in your slow cooker.
- When your chicken is cooked it will be fall-apart tender! I like to get mine out in one piece by sliding two spatulas or large mixing spoons underneath both ends of the chicken and then quickly lifting it up and out onto a dish. An alternative method is to create a foil or baking-paper sling under your chicken prior to cooking. This can be used to grasp and lift the chicken out at the end of cooking. This can be a large sling design or two strips crossed over to form a basket of sorts. Whatever works for you!

Help! I accidently cooked the absorbent pad from under my raw meat...

That awful moment when you first spot it… you have made a lovely slow cooker meal and you are just giving it a little stir before you serve it, when it appears: the absorbent pad from under your raw meat has accidentally ended up in your slow cooker – and *gasp* – you've cooked it!

Oh no!

What now?

Is your meal ruined?

Do you have to throw it out?

This actually happens a lot. More than you'd realise. At least a few times a week we see a member of our Facebook group looking for advice on what to do when they realise they've done this. So our goal was to get to the bottom of it and what it means for you and your pot full of otherwise yummy slow cooked food.

What are they?
Absorbent meat pads or absorbent meat soakers are the little packages that often sit between your raw meat and your butcher's tray. The purpose of the pad is to catch and absorb the liquid that naturally drains from raw meat and would otherwise pool in your meat tray and potentially spill out on you when it was tilted. It also helps prevent meat from sitting in a pool of raw meat juice that could breed bacteria and reduce shelf life.

The fact they are often black to begin with or soaked red with juices means that it's easier than you may think to tip your raw meat into your slow cooker from the tray without realising you have tipped in the pad as well.

What are they made of?
The butchers that I spoke to explained that the pads are usually made from paper pulp, plant fibres or non-toxic silicone with a plastic outer layer. They explained that they are approved for use in contact with food that is intended for human consumption, which means they have to be food-safe and non-toxic. They are not digestible, which means that even if you ate one it would go right through your digestive tract.

But what about when they are cooked? Does that change things?

Do I need to throw my meal in the bin?
The general consensus seems to be – if the pad is broken or pierced in any way, sadly yes, you should throw your meal out.

However, if the pad is intact you may decide to still eat your meal if you are comfortable doing so. A manufacturer of these pads (www.thermasorb.com.au) advises that if they are not broken then your meal is okay to eat. The poisons information hotline people agree. They report getting a lot of calls regarding this issue and advise that if the packet is broken your meal should be discarded just to be safe. However, in their experience, if the packet is intact most people will have no ill effects. From their experience, at worst those with a sensitive stomach may experience mild nausea or an unpleasant taste, but this is rare and most of their callers experience no ill effects.

So the choice is ultimately yours.

Help! My cream has split

In our slow cooking community we often see members posting their concern over split cream in their slow cooked dishes.

What is splitting?
A lot of people will refer to dairy products that have split as being 'curdled'. If your dairy product curdles during storage that's a problem and you should throw it out; don't use it. However, if it separates during cooking, it's more likely to be split and that is really only a change of appearance and texture. It's still perfectly fine to eat.

Why does it occur?
Sauces made with dairy products can split for several reasons.

- Low fat content – dairy products with high fat content are less likely to split.
- High heat – exposing dairy products to high heat, eg close to boiling, increases the likelihood of splitting.
- High acidity – adding dairy products to recipes with elevated acidic content can also cause splitting.

How can I prevent it?
- Choose higher-fat versions of your dairy product rather than the low fat varieties.
- If possible add the dairy product at the end of your cooking time rather than the beginning. You can even take it off the heat before you add it.
- When adding cream early, try whisking a teaspoon or so of cornflour into the cream first before adding it to your dish.
- Choose 'cooking cream' or 'creme fraiche' or double cream – these are less likely to split.
- Allow dairy products to come to room temperature before adding them. This can also help.
- Adding cream to a water-based recipe can cause splitting. Stirring regularly helps to avoid this.

What do I do once it's happened?
- Remember ... it's okay to eat. While a dish with split cream may not look perfect, it's certainly NOT a reason to throw it out!
- If the nature of the dish allows it, try giving the food a really good stir or whisk.
- Alternatively, try stirring through a little cornflour and water slurry.

Don't be discouraged! Next time just try the preventative measures. If all else fails, eat your meal with your eyes shut and you'll never know the difference *wink*.

Can I prepare a meal in advance and store it in the slow cooker bowl in my fridge overnight, then put it on the next morning?

Yes, you can if you wish. But it comes with risks!

Heating a cold bowl can lead to it cracking.

Also, the bowl and its contents will retain that cold for a long time and thus take even longer to reach safe temperatures once you begin cooking, placing you at increased risk of food poisoning.

A great way around this is to prepare the dish in advance but store it in the fridge in another large bowl, for example a mixing bowl. The food can then be poured into the slow cooker bowl in the morning. You still have all the convenience but without any of the risk.

What is the best way to clean my slow cooker bowl?

It happens to all of us sometimes! We finish cooking our recipe only to find a baked-on ring of cooked or burnt residue inside our slow cooker or on the base. Or maybe the inner casing of your slow cooker has stains in it? Don't despair – we've got the solution!

Basics
- The sooner you get it off the better!
- Avoid harsh abrasive chemicals or cleaning scourers.
- Always unplug the unit from the power source before cleaning.

Cleaning inside the cooking bowl

Most slow cooker bowls can simply be washed by hand in the sink. Some are okay for washing in the dishwasher. Be sure to check your manual for what is suitable for your model as not all models are dishwasher safe.

However, if you find yourself with a baked-on ring around the bowl that's hard to remove, the easiest way to get rid of it is remove the food, add water to a level above the baked-on ring and leave the slow cooker turned to LOW for a couple of hours. The ring should clean away much more easily then.

Some suggest placing a dishwasher tablet or even a denture cleaning tablet in the slow cooker while the water is heating in it for up to two hours but it is advisable to check with your user manual whether this is safe for your model.

Ceramic bowls and lids will not withstand sudden temperature changes. Do not fill the bowl with cold water when it is hot as it will crack.

Some ceramic bowls have a porous base and should not be left standing in water for extended periods because they might absorb water. It's fine to fill inside the bowl with water and leave it for any amount of time, but avoid leaving the entire bowl standing IN water.

Cleaning inside the main casing of the slow cooker

The metal housing of the slow cooker and electrical lead should NOT be placed in water! Be sure to completely unplug your unit from the power source and allow it to cool before any cleaning.

Over time you will find some of your food will splash down into the main casing of your slow cooker – under the cooking bowl.

It is important to ALWAYS CHECK YOUR INSTRUCTION MANUAL FIRST as to how your manufacturer recommends you clean your slow cooker.

Normally, electrical cables inside the base unit are fully sealed, but you should still exercise extreme caution in cleaning this main base unit – and again, never place the unit itself in water. If you can see heating elements inside the base do not clean or add water in this area and instead contact the manufacturer for advice.

For those who wish to proceed with cleaning inside the main casing, here are some suggestions I have gathered from members of the Slow Cooker Central community.

- Simply wipe the spill off with a soft, damp cloth and a small amount of dish detergent, especially if the spill is fresh or new.
- Clean using a mix of baking soda and vinegar on a cloth or sponge.
- Use a chalk-based cleaning paste like Gumption, which you can find in your supermarket cleaning aisle.
- Use baking soda and lemon juice. Combine and allow to foam then apply with a soft pad, sponge or scourer.
- While a soft green scrubbing type pad scourer should be okay, please think carefully before using a stronger steel wool type scourer as you could scratch your inner casing or bowl. A gentle sponge or rubber based scrubbing tool is ideal.
- Some report using a thin coat of oven cleaner (a fume-free version if you can), left for an hour or so then wiped off. If doing this I would recommend wiping over a few times with a damp cloth to minimise any smells next time you use the unit. Note: oven cleaners can be caustic and may even dissolve paint on the outside of your cooker, so use sparingly and cautiously.

Prevention is best
Rather than deal with the clean-up, try to prevent spills where you can!

- Spray your slow cooker bowl with some non-stick cooking spray before beginning.
- Line your slow cooker with baking paper for baked items or ones you think may stick.
- Use a slow-cooker liner bag or even an oven bag to slow-cook your dish.
- Follow the cooking time recommended in the recipe and avoid overcooking and burning.
- Do not overfill your slow cooker, which would increase the likelihood of spilling and staining in the casing area.

Are there any 'diet' recipes for slow cookers?

Almost every recipe can be adapted for weight loss or to make it healthier (with some obvious dessert-type exceptions).

Ways to adapt recipes to make them more waist-friendly include:

- Choose lean. Choose leaner cuts of meat than the recipe specifies. For example, go with low-fat mince, low-fat sausages or skinless chicken.
- Brown and bin. Brown meats before you slow cook them. This gives you an opportunity to drain and discard the fat rather than include it in your slow cooking recipe. Some people even like to boil their mince before cooking to remove fat.
- Trim the fat. Remove the fat before cooking, or remove fat or skin from the completed dish before serving.
- Bulk up. Add extra vegetables to your meal. If the dish you are cooking has few or no vegetables why not add some during cooking? Or when it comes to plating up your meal, load your plate with steamed or stir-fried veg to fill you up.
- Slash the salt. Choose low-sodium options for your ingredients. Even if the recipe doesn't specify it, I often change things like soy sauce or stocks to low-sodium options to cut the salt from the overall recipe.
- Choose low fat. In the same way that you can substitute low-salt ingredients, do the same with low-fat ones. Opt for low-fat yoghurts, milks and cheese, for example – pretty much anything that has a low-fat option.
- Selecting sides. What can make or break a meal when it comes to your waistline is sides. Choose wisely and your scales will thank you. Opt for healthier options like vegetables, salads and brown rice and the impact of the main meal is less.
- Portion power. Healthy eating is largely about moderation. You can enjoy that meal you really want, without having to totally overdo it. It's better to consume small portions of the foods that you crave rather than trying to resist them totally and ending up blowing out on a binge. Match the portion sizes of the various food groups on your plate with recommendations for a balanced and healthy diet.
- Love your leftovers. Why not cook extra when you do your next slow cooker meal? Then you can portion and store leftovers into healthy-sized meals all ready to take to work or to grab when the next attack of munchies strikes. It makes you less likely to make poor choices on impulse or opt for unhealthy take-away food.

- More of the same. As with all healthy eating plans, don't forget the basics. Drink plenty of water, eat mindfully, pack heaps of variety into your meal plans, choose fresh food when you can and move more!

Is it toxic to slow cook raw red kidney beans?

Yes, it is! But only raw beans. This does *not* include the canned varieties that are already cooked. A good explanation can be found at www.choosingvoluntarysimplicity.com:

'Raw kidney beans contain especially large amounts of [phytohaemagglutinin], and amazingly, eating just four or five raw or improperly cooked kidney beans can make a person extremely ill. Ingesting larger amounts can actually cause death. Other beans, including white kidney beans, broad beans and lima beans, contain the same toxin in smaller but still dangerous amounts.'

If you'd like to read further on this issue, these websites would be good starting points:

- www.choosingvoluntarysimplicity.com/crockpots-slow-cooking-dried-beans-phytohaemagglutinin/
- www.medic8.com/healthguide/food-poisoning/red-kidney-bean-toxins.html

Slow cooking cakes

Cooking cakes in slow cookers is out of the norm for a lot of traditionalist slow cooker users, so we wanted to include some advice on what can and can't be used in cake making in your slow cooker, and also to provide some general tips for getting the most out of your slow cooker cake making.

First and foremost, as detailed on page 11, the 'tea towel trick' is very important to prevent condensation dripping on your cakes when cooking them in the slow cooker.

Slow cookers can be used to cook packet (box) cake mixes as well as your own favourite from-scratch recipe.

But what do you cook the actual cake in?

There are three options.

1. Line your slow cooker inner bowl and cook your cake directly in it.
When doing this I find lining the bowl with non-stick baking paper not only prevents sticking but also gives you something to hold onto so you can lift the cake out at the end of the cooking time.

2. Cook your cake in a metal cake tin.
If you are concerned about using a metal cake tin dry in your slow cooker (ceramic bowls in particular are unsuitable for dry cooking) simply fill the bottom of the slow cooker bowl with 2–3 cm (1 in) of water first, then sit your cake tin gently in this water.

You can also elevate the cake tin off the bottom of the slow cooker to allow heat to circulate evenly around your cake. This can be achieved by resting the cake tin on a metal trivet, on metal egg rings or even on scrunched up balls of aluminium foil.

3. Cook your cake in a silicone cake tin.
Silicone cake tins (full size and cupcake size) are also safe to use in your slow cooker and will not melt. After all, they are intended for the high heat of conventional ovens.

When using non-ceramic slow cooker bowls I personally sit my silicone cake tins/cups directly onto the bottom of the slow cooker, without water, with no concerns. But if you prefer, you can elevate your tin using the methods described above. When using a ceramic cooker bowl I again add water first.

As with all non-traditional slow cooking, be sure to check your manual first and only do what you are comfortable doing.

Slow cooker fudge FAQs

Our members LOVE cooking fudge! We have hundreds of different varieties on the website, so you can browse for fudge online or use one of the recipes in this book. I've compiled some commonly asked questions about fudge to help you along the way.

What type of chocolate can I use?
Any type. Change the flavour of the chocolate to change the taste of the fudge. Milk chocolate, white chocolate, hazelnut chocolate, cookies and cream chocolate … the options are unlimited. Some members use cooking chocolate,

but others say the taste is not the same, so use your judgement. (Cooking chocolate does tend to melt at higher temperatures, so regular chocolate is ideal for the lower temp of the slow cooker.) If you are using chocolate that has a liquid-type filling, eg Caramello, you will need to increase the chocolate amount to account for this.

Can I add chocolate and lollies to my fudge

Yes. You can mix or top your fudge with anything you like. Make the base fudge, stir through whatever you like to add, then pour it into the lined tin to set. For example, you could add chopped nuts, biscuits, Mars bars, lollies (candies) … whatever you like. Or pour your fudge into your tray to set then decorate the surface with these types of toppings. Again the options are endless.

How do I actually cook it? Do I need to stir it?

Break up the chocolate and place it in your slow cooker. Pour over condensed milk and add the butter and vanilla. LEAVE THE LID OFF your slow cooker and turn it on low and walk away. Every 10–15 minutes just pass by and give it a stir. It's that easy. As you near the end of the cooking time you may need to keep a closer eye on it but really it's just the odd stir along the way and there is nothing else to do.

Can I use any spoon to stir?

It's ideal to use a metal or silicone spoon when stirring your fudge. A wooden spoon can absorb some of the liquid from your fudge so it's best to avoid these. (Not to mention the fact that a metal spoon is a little nicer to lick clean!)

My fudge has seized – how can I fix it?

If things don't go to plan, your fudge might seize, which means it turns hard and weird instead of glossy. This problem can result from water getting into the fudge – remember, lids off for fudge to avoid condensation drips. Using a wooden spoon can do the same – remember, use a metal, plastic or silicone spoon for stirring fudge. There are a few approaches our members use to rescue seized fudge. Try stirring the living daylights out of it to bring it back to glossy. Others add a little splash of milk or condensed milk or even a bit more chocolate then stir like the clappers to bring it all back together. All is not lost. This is fixable – stir stir stir!

How do I know when it's done?
Everyone's slow cooker takes a different amount of time to cook. Simply melting the chocolate is not enough. After some time, you'll notice a very slight 'crust' on the surface as you stir, and the mixture will come away from the edges of the bowl slightly. This is the best sign that it's done. Some larger (hotter) machines may achieve this in half an hour. My 1.5 litre cooker that I use for fudge takes more like 90 minutes to achieve this. You will get to know yours.

What do I do with it once it's cooked?
Stir through any extras you want to add, then pour your fudge into a slice tray (I use one approximately 20cm x 20cm) lined with baking paper. You can use silicone moulds instead if you choose. Smooth the surface down to flat and add any decorations you like. If nothing is being added then simply place your tray in the fridge until set – approximately four hours should do it. Then use the baking paper to lift out your fudge from the tray. Remove the paper and cut the fudge quickly. Dipping your knife into hot water first can help cut cleanly.

How should I store my fudge?
Store your fudge in a sealed container in the fridge (make it a non-transparent container if you want to keep it from being rapidly gobbled up by the fudge fanatics in your home *wink*). The fudge will keep up to four weeks in a fridge. It can also be frozen for up to three months.

My fudge didn't set. What did I do wrong?
Please review the above tips. One of them will most likely reveal the reason your fudge did not set. You could also try returning your fudge to the slow cooker to reheat, adding more chocolate, then cooking it for longer. Not using enough chocolate is the number one cause of fudge not setting.

Pantry staples

One of the best ways to ease into trying new recipes is to have a supply of staple items in your pantry – on hand and at the ready for your next kitchen session. Build up your collection and all future recipes will be even friendlier on your budget.

Useful staples include:

- Baking powder
- Balsamic vinegar
- Canned or dried fruits
- Canned or dried vegetables
- Canned soups: condensed cream soups in various flavours (especially cream of mushroom and cream of chicken)
- Coconut cream and milk
- Cornflour
- Couscous
- Curry powder
- Dry packet soups such as French onion and chicken noodle
- Flour: plain (all-purpose) and self-raising
- Garlic: fresh or minced in jar
- Ginger: fresh or minced in jar
- Gravy powder/granules
- Herbs and spices: fresh in your garden, frozen in tubes or dried in jars and packets – as many as you can gather!
- Honey
- Lentils
- Mustard powder
- Parmesan: fresh or dried
- Pasta
- Pepper
- Powdered milk or UHT milk
- Rice
- Salt
- Sauces: sweet chilli, BBQ, tomato, worcestershire, soy, mint, oyster, hoisin
- Stock: powder, cubes or long life liquid (especially beef, chicken and vegetable)
- Sugar: brown and white
- Sweetened condensed milk
- Tinned tomatoes
- Tinned tuna
- Tomato paste
- Vinegar
- Wine: red and white
- Yeast

This is by no means an exhaustive list but it's a great start!

Goodbye, oven. Hello slow cooker! Converting oven and stovetop recipes for your slow cooker

Now you're hooked on slow cooking, I bet you'll find there are heaps of your family's favourite recipes that you have always cooked in the oven or on the stovetop that you want to convert for a slow cooker. And, for almost all of them, there is no reason you can't!

Here are some simple pointers:

- Reduce the amount of liquid. The condensation that forms in your slow cooker when in use means that recipes cooked in slow cookers need much less liquid then their traditional stovetop or oven counterparts. As a general rule try reducing the total liquid by approximately one quarter.
- Use cheaper cuts of meat. Remember that almost any cut of meat – even the cheapest and toughest – is sure to be tender after slow cooking. So feel free to replace more expensive cuts of meat with a cheaper option.
- Adjust the amounts of herbs and spices. Many people recommend reducing them by one half when converting a regular recipe for a slow cooker.
- Adjust the time. See the chart below to convert your stove and oven times to slow cooker times.
- Arrange the ingredients. When filling your slow cooker, put the root vegetables around the bottom and sides of your slow cooker, then place your meat on top.
- Take notes and experiment. It may take some trial and error to tweak your old favourites but it'll be worth it. Adjust liquids as you go (adding or removing) and keep an eye on cooking times. Take notes as you try new things so you'll always know just what worked the best for you. Soon you'll have a recipe you can use anywhere!

Stovetop & Oven Cooking Times	Slow Cooking on LOW Cooking Times	Slow Cooking on HIGH Cooking Times
15–30 mins	4–6 hours	1½–2½ hours
45 mins–1 hour	6½–8 hours	3–4 hours
1½–2½ hours	9–12 hours	4½–6 hours
3–5 hours	12½–18 hours	5–7 hours

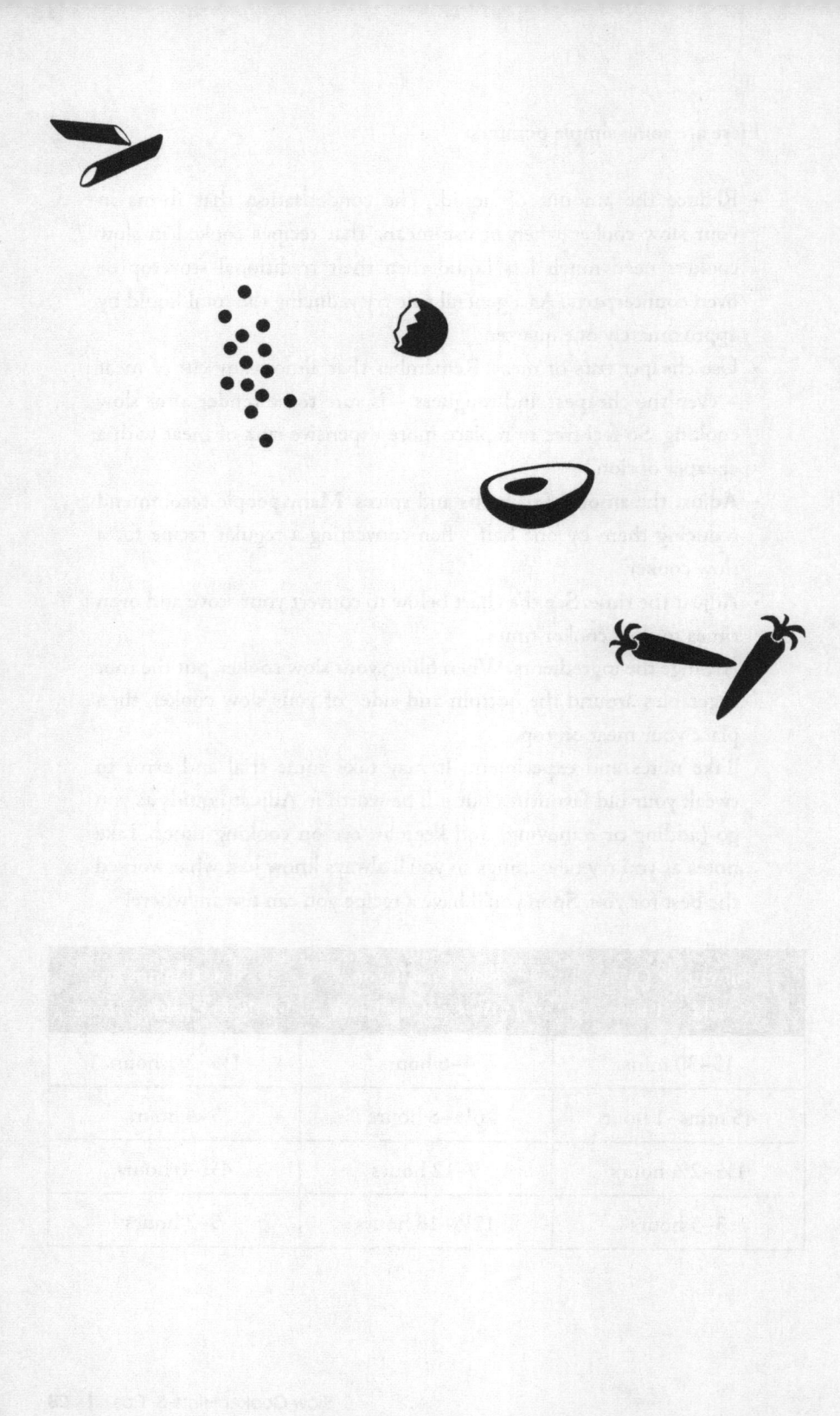

BABY & TODDLER

BABY & TODDLER

Puréed Veg for 6+ Months

Fresh for baby!

Serves lots! • Preparation 10 mins • Cook 5 hours • Cooker capacity 5 litres

- 3 small sweet potatoes
- 2 potatoes
- ¼ pumpkin
- 3 carrots
- 5 mushrooms
- 1 cup peas
- ½ cup corn kernels
- 1 head broccoli
- 1 apple

1. Peel and dice all the ingredients. Place into the slow cooker with 1 cup water.
2. Cover and cook on HIGH for 5 hours. Stir occasionally and add additional water if required, though the veggies don't need to be covered with water.
3. Cool then purée until smooth. Divide into serving portions, and freeze.

Jessica Lindsay

Chicken, Avocado & Broccoli

As a first-time mum, I had a lot of trouble introducing solids to my baby. After reading up a bit on baby-led weaning I decided to give that a go. I learnt pasta was great for babies and toddlers; it's simple and easy. I figured if I added a bit of cooking cream and fresh vegetables in the slow cooker I can make my own pasta sauces. I have tried many concoctions but chicken, avocado and broccoli has definitely been the winner.

Serves 4 • Preparation 15 mins • Cook 5 hours • Cooker capacity 5 litres

2 chicken breast fillets
2 avocados
1 cup cooking cream
150 g (5½ oz) broccoli, cut into florets
Pasta or rice, to serve

1. Combine the chicken, avocado and cooking cream in the slow cooker.
2. Cover and cook on LOW for 4 hours.
3. Add the broccoli and cook, covered, for a further 1 hour.
4. Serve with pasta or rice.

Jessica Goodyer

Babies' Savoury Veggies with Couscous

As Mum to four young children I needed to find a way to feed my baby economically and easily. Doing this in the slow cooker meant I could get it all in the pot and walk away, knowing I was giving him the nutrition (with no store-bought preservatives) that he needed, AND the time!

Makes 11 cups • Preparation 15 mins • Cook 4 hours • Cooker capacity 6 litres

- 1 pumpkin (about the size of side plate)
- 1 parsnip
- 2 potatoes
- 2 big carrots
- 1 big handful of spinach
- 2 sweet potatoes
- ½ head of broccoli
- 2 large apples
- 2 teaspoons chicken stock powder
- ½ cup couscous

1. Peel, deseed, and chop all veggies as required. The smaller it's chopped the quicker it will cook. I chopped mine into fingerprint sized pieces.
2. Add to the slow cooker with the stock powder and enough water to submerge the vegetables.
3. Cover and cook on HIGH for 4 hours, until the vegetables are soft enough to mash.
4. Stir in the couscous. Put lid back on and turn off slow cooker. Leave to soften couscous and cool slightly.
5. Purée mixture in a food processor until smooth. Divide into serving portions, and freeze any that won't be used within a day or two.

Debbie Manteiga

Baby Food – Apple with Cinnamon

Apple purée is an ideal baby food as it's easy to digest. Pink lady and royal gala apples are best as they are sweet and not too tart. One of the apples may be replaced with a ripe pear. Leftovers may be frozen in ice cube trays for later use. Older kids or adults can also enjoy this as a dessert with a scoop of ice-cream.

Serves 5 portions as baby food • Preparation 5 mins
Cook 2 hours • Cooker capacity 1.5 litres

5 large pink lady apples
Pinch of ground cinnamon (optional)

1. Peel and core apples, and chop roughly. Place into the slow cooker with 2 tablespoons water and the cinnamon (if using).
2. Cover and cook on HIGH for two hours, stirring once or twice during cooking.
3. Mash with back of spoon when soft, or purée in a food processor.

Tennille Langley

Babies Blue Brekky

I made this for my little girl when she first went on to solids, as I wanted to know what was in her food.

Serves 12 • Preparation 5 mins • Cook 4–5 hours • Cooker capacity 1.5 litres

1 banana
1 apple
1 handful blueberries
¼ cup rice
½ handful rolled oats

1. Peel and chop the banana and apple. Combine with the other ingredients and 1½ cups water in the slow cooker.
2. Cover and cook on LOW for 4–5 hours or until rice is soft. Stir a few times during cooking. Purée and pass through a sieve.

NOTE: This didn't freeze well unfortunately. Keep in the fridge for up to 3 days.

Samantha Carter

BREAKFAST

BREAKFAST

Easy Mixed Beans

This recipe is so easy the kids can make it themselves.

Serves 8 • Preparation 5 mins • Cook 3–4 hours • Cooker capacity 6 litres

5 x 420 g (15 oz) cans 5 bean mix, rinsed and drained
300 g (10½ oz) jar medium (or mild if you prefer) chunky salsa
⅓ cup brown sugar

1. Combine all the ingredients in the slow cooker.
2. Cover and cook on LOW for 3–4 hours.

NOTE: These are delicious just with toast or can be added to a full cooked breakfast. Fried diced bacon can also be added for extra flavour.

Fiona Masters

Morning Mushrooms

Imagine a big tasty mushroom filled with garlic butter, bacon, tomato, spinach and topped with melted tasty cheese! You can vary the fillings to fit your taste.

Makes 2 • Preparation 10 mins • Cook 1 hour • Cooker capacity 6 litres

- 2 large flat mushrooms
- 2 teaspoons garlic butter (or add your own minced garlic to regular butter)
- 4 cherry tomatoes, diced
- 6 baby spinach leaves, cut into strips
- 50 g diced bacon
- ½ cup grated tasty cheese

1. Line the slow cooker with baking paper. Gently remove the stalk from the mushrooms.
2. Top the mushrooms with garlic butter, tomato, spinach and bacon. Carefully place into the slow cooker. Sprinkle cheese onto the mushroom topping.
3. Cover, putting a tea towel (dish towel) under the lid, and cook on HIGH for 45 minutes–1 hour, until the mushroom is cooked and cheese has melted.

Paulene Christie

Breakfast Casserole

A fully loaded breakfast sure to satisfy! I used to take a lot of time making big breakfasts for the family on special occasions, so I wanted something I could quickly put together. The kids enjoy helping me make it too! It is a great dish to add leftovers to as well.

Serves 6–10 • Preparation 15 mins • Cook 2½ hours • Cooker capacity 6 litres

500 g (1 lb 2 oz) potato gems
1½ cups grated tasty cheese
6 cooked and chopped sausages (or bacon rashers)
1 onion, sliced
¼ cup HP sauce
1½ tablespoons Worcestershire sauce
4 tomatoes, sliced
6 eggs
200 g (7 oz) feta cheese, crumbled

1. Line the slow cooker with baking paper. Make a layer of potato gems on the bottom and sprinkle with a thin layer of cheese.
2. Add the sausages and onion, and drizzle with the sauces. Make a layer of tomato slices and season with salt and pepper. Crack the eggs over the top and sprinkle with more grated cheese, then the feta.
3. Cover, putting a tea towel (dish towel) under the lid, and cook on HIGH for 2½ hours.

Melinda Boddington

Caz's Fish Finger Brekky Bake

This recipe is delicious and the whole family will love it. So easy for the kids to make. You can also have it cold with a fresh salad for a quick and easy lunch.

Serves 4–6 • Preparation 30 mins • Cook 1½–2 hours • Cooker capacity 5 litres

20 fish fingers
2 tomatoes, diced
1 onion, diced
8 eggs, lightly beaten
½ cup cream
1 cup grated tasty cheese

1. Line a slow cooker with baking paper. Arrange the fish fingers in a single layer on the paper. Spread the tomato and onion evenly over the fish fingers.
2. Combine the eggs, cream and half the cheese in a bowl and season with salt and pepper. Pour over the fish fingers.
3. Cover, putting a tea towel (dish towel) under the lid, and cook on HIGH for 1½–2 hours. 5 minutes before serving, sprinkle the remaining cheese over the top.

NOTE: If you want you can also add chopped bacon and/or capsicum (peppers).

Carol Wilkinson

Cheesy Mushroom, Bacon & Onion Eggy Breakfast Slice

On busy school or sport mornings this is a great breakfast to eat on the run. You could cook it the night before and grab a cold slice from the fridge or reheat and away you go. It's also yummy for school lunchboxes or mess-free travel meals on the road.

Serves 4 • Preparation 15 mins • Cook 1¼ hours • Cooker capacity 6 litres

Spray oil
1 cup grated tasty cheese
8 eggs, lightly beaten
2 large mushrooms, diced
½ onion, diced
125 g (4½ oz) diced bacon

1. Spray a silicone flan case with spray oil, or line your slow cooker directly with baking paper and spray with oil.
2. Spread ½ cup of the cheese on the bottom of the flan case or paper so that when the cooked slice is inverted onto a serving plate the cheese is on top.
3. Combine the eggs, mushroom, onion, bacon and remaining cheese, then pour into the flan case or onto the paper.
4. Cover, putting a tea towel (dish towel) under the lid, and cook on HIGH for 1¼ hours, or until egg has set.
5. Invert onto a plate and cut into slices to serve.

Paulene Christie

Easy Cheesy Breakfast Beans

Perfect for a lazy Sunday morning or even a lunch treat. These easy cheesy beans are devoured by our kids! They are perfect served on their own or with a side of buttery toast triangles.

Serves 5 • Preparation 5 mins • Cook 2¼ hours • Cooker capacity 6 litres

6 skinless frankfurts, cut into chunks
2 x 440 g (15½ oz) cans baked beans in your favourite flavour (BBQ sauce is ours)
1 cup grated tasty cheese

1. Add the frankfurts to the slow cooker then the beans.
2. Cover and cook on LOW for 1 hour 45 minutes or until everything is piping hot. Sprinkle the top with the grated cheese and cook for a further 30 minutes, until melted.

NOTE: You could brown some diced bacon or onion and add that too. Diced mushroom, tomatoes or capsicum (pepper) would also be a yummy addition.

Paulene Christie

Scrambled Eggs

This is a basic scrambled egg recipe, and other things can be added like chopped bacon, herbs or spring onions (scallions) if you wish.

Serves 2 • Preparation 5 mins • Cook 1¼ hours • Cooker capacity 3 litres

5 eggs
½ cup milk
20 g (¾ oz) butter

1. Lightly whisk the eggs with a fork. Add the milk and mix well. Place all ingredients into the slow cooker with the butter, and season with salt and pepper.
2. Cover and cook on HIGH for 1¼ hours, lightly whisking every 15 minutes until eggs have set.

Karen Stuckings

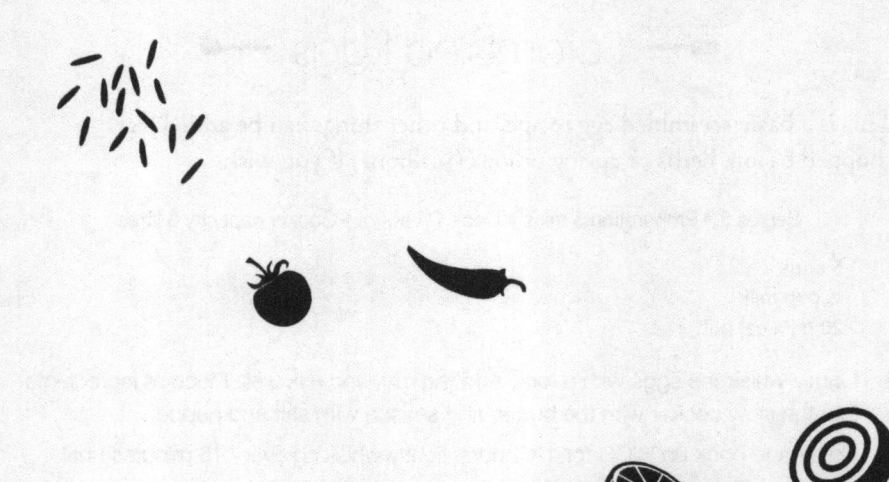

SUPER SIDES

SUPER SIDES

Brown Rice

Our kids prefer brown rice to white and it's a bonus that it's better for them. If your kids love brown too then this is a great easy way to cook it as a side dish. This gives a sticky rice result (like sticky sushi rice consistency), not as dry and fluffy as stove rice, but still tender and tasty and perfect for little ones to keep on their spoon!

Makes 2½ cups cooked rice • Preparation 5 mins • Cook 2 hours • Cooker capacity 1.5 litres

Spray oil
1 cup brown rice

1. Spray the slow cooker bowl with oil. Add the rice and 2 cups warm tap water.
2. Cover and cook on HIGH for 1 hour 45 minutes. Do not open the lid during cooking time. Turn off the slow cooker and leave the rice to steam for a further 15 minutes.
3. Season and serve as desired.

NOTE: If you use a larger slow cooker than the 1.5 litre it will cook hotter. Check during cooking as it may need less time or additional water.

Paulene Christie

4 Ingredient Potato Bake

A no cream, no milk quick and easy potato bake with only 4 ingredients.

Serves 4–6 • Preparation 10 mins • Cook 5 hours • Cooker capacity 5.5 litres

500 g (1 lb 2 oz) potatoes, cut into 5 mm (¼ inch) slices
400 g (14 oz) mozzarella, sliced, plus 1 cup grated
450 g (15½ oz) ham, sliced
2 teaspoons thyme leaves

1. Make alternating layers of potatoes, sliced mozzarella and ham in the slow cooker, finishing with a layer of potatoes.
2. Cover and cook on LOW for 4 hours.
3. Combine the grated mozzarella and thyme leaves and sprinkle over the top of potatoes. Cover, putting a tea towel (dish towel) under the lid, and cook on HIGH for a further 1 hour.

NOTE: Mozzarella can be replaced with dairy-free or lactose-free cheese of your choice.

Felicity Barnett

Slow Cooker Corn

No more boring corn when this is made. It's juicy, full of flavour and something the whole family will love.

Serves 4–6 • Preparation 5 mins • Cook 4–6 hours • Cooker capacity minimum 3 litres

- 1 kg (2 lb 3 oz) frozen corn cobs or 4 fresh corn cobs
- 1 teaspoon ground turmeric
- 1 teaspoon garlic powder
- 1 teaspoon ground paprika
- 1 teaspoon curry powder
- 2 x 400 g cans coconut milk

1. Place the corn cobs into the slow cooker and add the spices on top. Pour the coconut milk over.
2. Cover and cook on LOW for 4–6 hours.

NOTE: You can halve the coconut milk if you don't want much liquid, though it is delicious used as a soup or curry base. I've added peas towards the end but you don't have to do this.

Megan Macleod

Baked Baby Potatoes

These are a great side dish to your next BBQ or main meal, or even great tossed through a salad. Our kids often like to serve these cut open with a dollop of butter or sauce on top (you know what kids are like with their sauce!).

Serves 5 • Preparation 5 mins • Cook 3 hours • Cooker capacity 6 litres

- 10 small whole baby washed potatoes
- 1–2 tablespoons olive oil
- Good pinch Himalayan pink rock salt
- Good pinch cracked black pepper
- 2 teaspoons chopped chives
- 1 teaspoon chopped fresh parsley

1. Place the potatoes into the slow cooker. Drizzle olive oil over the potatoes and season with salt and pepper.
2. Cover and cook on LOW for 3 hours.
3. Test potatoes with fork to ensure they are tender. Remove from slow cooker and place in a bowl, add the fresh herbs and season with more salt and pepper if you like. Toss to coat.

NOTE: If you use larger potatoes you will need to increase cooking time to ensure they are cooked until tender.

Paulene Christie

Creamy Potatoes

My daughter loves how the potatoes turn out in our One Pot Chicken Dinner (in the *Super Savers* book) so I wanted to try and do something with potatoes that would be like them. This is what we came up with – melt in your mouth potatoes. She says they are like mash without having to mash!

Serves 4–6 • Preparation 10 mins • Cook 7–8 hours • Cooker capacity 3.5 litres

- 500 g (1 lb 2 oz) small potatoes, quartered
- ½ leek, finely sliced
- 4 garlic cloves, sliced
- 2 bay leaves
- 6 sprigs thyme (remove leaves and discard stems)
- Pinch cracked black pepper
- ½ cup cream
- 1 tablespoon cornflour (cornstarch)
- 1 cup vegetable stock

1. Place the potatoes into the slow cooker. Add the leek, garlic, herbs and pepper.
2. Mix the cream and cornflour together in a jug and pour over the potatoes. Rinse the jug with the stock and add to the slow cooker.
3. Cover and cook on LOW for 7–8 hours.

NOTE: This can also be served cold as a potato salad.

Felicity Barnett and Susannah Durbidge

Mexican Rice

This is my spin on a Mexican rice dish, which I adapted for a slow cooker. I hope you enjoy it as much as my family does. It's a spicy rice dish which can be eaten on its own or as an accompaniment to other dishes. Great with poultry or fish.

Serves 4 • Preparation 20 mins • Cook 3½ hours • Cooker capacity 5 litres

- 5 tomatoes, chopped
- 1 brown onion, chopped
- ⅓ cup vegetable oil
- 3 cups basmati rice
- 5 garlic cloves, sliced
- 1 vegetable stock cube, crumbled
- 435 g (15½ oz) can refried beans
- 1–2 tablespoons dried coriander (cilantro) leaves
- 1 tablespoon tomato paste (concentrated purée)
- 1 teaspoon ground coriander
- ¼ teaspoon salt
- ¼ teaspoon pepper
- ⅛ teaspoon dried chilli flakes
- ¼ cup lime juice

1. Combine the onion and tomatoes in a food processor and process to a pulp. Heat the oil in a large saucepan and sauté the rice and garlic for 2-3 minutes. Add the tomato mixture, stock cube and 4 cups boiling water. Let it bubble away for 5 minutes then pour into the slow cooker.
2. Stir in the remaining ingredients, except for the lime juice.
3. Cover and cook on HIGH for 3½ hours or until all the liquid is absorbed.
4. Stir in the lime juice and serve.

NOTE: If you have small children I would leave out the chilli flakes.

Tracey Ramsey

Caribbean Rice

As a health conscious mum I like to include fruit and veggies in my son's diet, without a struggle to get him to eat. We love rice so I thought: OK, let's make a fruity rice salad, add a few veggies and serve with BBQ meat. This is perfect for a beautiful Australian summer evening.

Serves 6 • Preparation 15 mins • Cook 3–4 hours • Cooker capacity 5 litre

2 cups white basmati rice
2½ cups water
1½ cups orange juice

SALAD INGREDIENTS
200 g (7 oz) pineapple cubes
12 cherry tomatoes, halved
¼ white or red onion, finely diced
¼ cup chopped mint
¼ cup chopped parsley
¼ cup chopped coriander

SALAD DRESSING
3 teaspoons extra virgin olive oil
2 teaspoons orange juice
1 teaspoon lime juice
1 finely diced red chilli, seeds removed (optional)
Pinch of sugar

1. Place the rice into a sieve and wash under cold running water. Drain. Place into the slow cooker with the water and orange juice.
2. Cover and cook on LOW for 3–4 hours, until rice is tender. Put aside to cool slightly.
3. Combine the salad ingredients, and whisk the salad dressing ingredients together. Toss salad and dressing through the rice and season with salt and pepper.

NOTE: You can serve warm or cold, but I suggest 'almost' cold rice, as kids often prefer warmish sides.

Laura Thomson

Caz's Mashed Potato

This recipe is just the absolute best we have ever had. It is so thick and creamy. The whole family loves it.

Serves 4–6 • Preparation 20 minutes • Cook 2–3 hours • Cooker capacity 3 litres

- 6 potatoes, cubed
- 1 onion, finely diced
- 2 teaspoons beef stock powder (see note)
- 60 g (2 oz) butter
- 1 cup cream (less if spuds are small)

1. Place the potatoes and onion in the slow cooker. Mix the stock powder with 3 cups water and pour over.
2. Cover and cook on HIGH for 2–3 hours. Test with a knife after 2 hours to see if they are ready – they should be falling apart.
3. Drain well, add the butter and cream and mash thoroughly for about 5 minutes. Whip with a fork until fluffy. Season with salt and pepper.

NOTE: I use beef stock if serving with red meat. I use chicken stock for white meat, and you can also use vegetable stock which goes well with silverside.

Carol Wilkinson

Cauliflower Cheese

This is a quick and easy cauliflower cheese with flavour to die for.

Serves 4–6 • Preparation time 10 mins • Cook 2½ hours • Cooker capacity 5.5 litres

300 ml (10 fl oz) cooking cream
1 tablespoon cornflour (cornstarch)
1 cauliflower, cut into florets
300 g (10½ oz) triple cream brie, skin removed, chopped
½ teaspoon minced garlic

1. Mix the cream and cornflour in a small bowl until smooth. Combine in the slow cooker with the remaining ingredients and season with salt and pepper.
2. Cover and cook on LOW for 2½ hours.

NOTE: The triple cream brie is quite mild in comparison to camembert cheese. So if you're wanting a stronger taste, use camembert. You could up the amount of garlic if you like (I'm a bit wimpy with garlic).

Denise Roberts

Tomato Sauce

Easy, versatile, everyday tomato sauce. This is a recipe I used to do on the stove but that involved peeling tomatoes and after developing problems with my hands it was no longer possible. I decided to do the same recipe in the slow cooker without peeling the tomatoes and see how it went. It turned out better than I could have hoped for and I make many jars every summer for use throughout the year, on pasta, as a pizza sauce and as an addition to vegetable soup.

Makes 6–8 jars • Preparation 30 mins • Cook 4 hours • Cooker capacity 6 litres

3 kg (6 lb 9 oz) tomatoes, chopped
500 g (1 lb 2 oz) jar tomato paste
1 bunch basil
3 tablespoons sugar
1 tablespoon salt

1. Place all the ingredients into the slow cooker.
2. Cover and cook on HIGH for 4 hours.
3. Blend until as smooth or chunky as you desire. Spoon into jars that have been washed well in hot soapy water then rinsed well.
4. Place lids onto the jars and put the jars into a large pot. Cover with water (jars should be submerged), bring to the boil and let simmer for 45 minutes. Allow to cool before removing jars from pot. Label and store in pantry ready for use.

Melissa Walton

Asian Greens

This is a great side dish to your next Chinese style dinner at home. Perfect for serving with fried rice and honey chicken, or the sweet and sour pork recipe from our previous books. It is a great way to get some nutrient-rich greens into your children but with flavour enough to keep them keen.

Serves 5 • Preparation 5 mins • Cook 1 hour 10 minutes • Cooker capacity 6 litres

2 teaspoons salt-reduced soy sauce
1 teaspoon minced garlic
1 teaspoon minced ginger
1 teaspoon sesame oil
1 bunch buk choy
1 bunch baby pak choy

1. Combine the soy sauce, garlic, ginger and sesame oil with 1 cup hot water in the slow cooker.
2. Trim the tough ends from the greens, separating the leaves as you do so. Stand leaves up in the slow cooker with the stems down towards the base. If they won't stand up just lay them in the cooker.
3. Cover and cook on HIGH for 1 hour 10 minutes, stirring halfway through if you are around. The greens will wilt as they cook so you'll soon have plenty of room in the cooker.
4. Stir the greens through the liquids well to coat. Drain then serve immediately.

Paulene Christie

SNACKS & LUNCHBOX

Sticky Chicken Wings

This is a lovely dish with great flavour and the meat is so tender it just falls off the bone.

Serves 6 • Preparation 5 mins • Cook 5 hours • Cooker capacity 5.5 litres

2 kg (4 lb 6 oz) chicken wings
½ cup soy sauce
½ cup brown sugar
⅓ cup balsamic vinegar
⅓ cup honey
¼ cup sweet chilli sauce
3 teaspoons minced garlic
1 teaspoon pepper
2 tablespoons cornflour (cornstarch)
2 tablespoons sesame seeds

1. Place the chicken wings into the slow cooker.
2. Mix the soy sauce, sugar, vinegar, honey, sweet chilli sauce, garlic and pepper together. Pour over the wings.
3. Cover and cook on LOW for 5 hours.
4. Take chicken from slow cooker and set aside. Mix the cornflour and 2 tablespoons water in a small bowl until smooth. Stir into the sauce to thicken, then return wings to sauce.
5. Serve wings sprinkled with sesame seeds.

Lynda Eagleson

Caz's Easy Peasy Sausage Rolls

These are so yummy for a quick lunch or even dinner with salad and fries. They're quick and easy to make, and budget friendly. Everyone loves sausage rolls and these are great for parties. Just cut them into bite sized pieces. Or make skewers out of them with pineapple, capsicum etc.

Serves 4–6 • Preparation 30 mins • Cook time 1½–2 hours • Cooker capacity 5 litres

6 sheets frozen puff pastry
Tomato sauce (ketchup), to taste
Dried mixed herbs, to taste
12 thin sausages
Oil, for greasing
Milk, for brushing
Sesame seeds (optional), for sprinkling

1. Cut each pastry sheet in half. Spread with the tomato sauce, leaving about 2.5 cm (1 inch) bare along one edge to seal. Sprinkle with the herbs.
2. Prick the sausages with a fork to stop them from bursting open. Roll up in the pastry. Lightly grease the slow cooker with oil and arrange the sausage rolls seam side down over the base in a single layer.
3. Brush pastry with a little milk and sprinkle with sesame seeds, if using.
4. Cover, putting a tea towel (dish towel) under the lid, and cook on HIGH for 1½–2 hours, until cooked through.

NOTE: You could also boil the sausages and peel off the skin if you like. Or roll them up without sauce or herbs, as an alternative.

Carol Wilkinson

Egg & Mayo Pasties

These flaky pastry pillows are filled with a creamy egg and mayo filling. Great for breakfast on the run, a light snack or lunchboxes. The curry flavour is very subtle and not too hot for children. However, if you are unsure or don't like curry flavour, you can leave it out.

Makes 8 • Preparation 30 mins • Cook 1 hour 10 mins • Cooker capacity 7 litres

Spray oil
6 eggs, hard-boiled
⅓ cup mayonnaise
1 tablespoon chopped chives or garlic chives
¼ teaspoon mild curry powder
2 sheets frozen puff pastry, just thawed
1 egg, lightly beaten

1. Line the slow cooker bottom with a sheet of baking paper and spray lightly with oil. Peel the eggs and place into a bowl. Use a fork to mash them, then mix in the mayo, chives and curry powder.
2. Cut each sheet of pastry into 4 squares. Place a triangle of egg mixture onto one half of each square. Fold the other half of the pastry square to enclose filling and form a triangle shaped pillow. Press the join with a fork to seal.
3. Arrange the pasties in a single layer in the slow cooker, and lightly brush top of each one with the egg.
4. Cover, putting a tea towel (dish towel) under the lid, and cook on HIGH for 35 minutes. Turn pasties over and brush the other side with egg. Cover (replace tea towel) and cook for a further 35 minutes.
5. Serve these hot and fresh, or cool and wrap in foil for lunchboxes.

NOTE: I use a large 7 litre cooker for this but if yours is smaller you may need to cook them in two batches if they won't all fit.

Paulene Christie

Tuna Patties

This is a recipe that I would normally shallow-fry, but I wanted to make them a little healthier. I decided to try them in the slow cooker and they worked. The other advantage is that you don't have to watch them closely like you do when frying.

Makes 8 • Preparation 10 mins • Cook 2 hours • Cooker capacity 7 litres

- 425 g (15 oz) can tuna in springwater, drained
- 1½ cups cold mashed potato (I used leftovers which included butter and cream)
- 2 teaspoons dried mixed herbs
- Finely grated rind of 1 lemon (optional)
- ½ onion, finely chopped
- 1 cup toasted breadcrumbs

1. Place the tuna, potato, herbs, lemon rind and onion into a mixing bowl. Season with freshly ground black pepper and mix well. Divide mixture into 8 patties.
2. Spread the breadcrumbs onto a plate and press each patty into the breadcrumbs to coat evenly. Line the slow cooker with baking paper, and place the patties onto the paper.
3. Cover, putting a tea towel (dish towel) under the lid, and cook on HIGH for 2 hours, turning once.

NOTE: I make my own breadcrumbs. Preheat the oven to 200°C (400°F) and line an oven tray with baking paper. Pulse 2 slices of wholemeal bread (with seeds) in a food processor until crumbs form. Spread out on prepared tray and bake for 5 minutes or until lightly toasted. Allow to cool before using.

Karen Stuckings

Mango Chutney Chicken Wings

2, 4, 6, 8! Tuck in – don't wait!! These wings are seriously THAT good, you'll be lining up for seconds from your slow cooker! A sure fire hit with the kids, and great for parties and entertaining.

Serves 4–6 • Preparation 10 mins • Cook 4 hours • Cooker capacity 6 litres

1 kg (2 lb 3 oz) chicken wings, tips removed if you prefer
250 g (9 oz) jar mango chutney
2 tablespoons oyster sauce
1 tablespoon Worcestershire sauce
1 tablespoon yellow mustard
1 teaspoon mild curry powder

1. Place the chicken wings into the slow cooker. Combine all the other ingredients and pour over the wings.
2. Cover and cook on low for 4 hours.

NOTE: If you are around during cooking time, gently move the wings around in the sauce or baste halfway through cooking to ensure they all get covered in the sauce for rich colour and taste.

Paulene Christie

Crumbed Chicken Nuggets

Who doesn't love chicken nuggets, especially home-made? No frying, so once the chicken is cut up the kids can make these themselves. They need to cook in a single layer so I cook in 2 batches and we eat the first batch while the second one cooks, or you could halve the recipe.

Makes 20 • Preparation 15 mins • Cook 2 hours • Cooker capacity 5.5 litres

¼ cup plain (all-purpose) flour
2 eggs, lightly beaten
1½ cups toasted breadcrumbs (see note)
2 teaspoons chicken stock powder
400 g (14 oz) chicken breasts, cut into pieces (try to make them the same size and thickness)

1. Place the flour into a freezer bag or a bowl. Place the egg in a separate bowl.
2. Combine the breadcrumbs and stock powder in a separate freezer bag or bowl.
3. First coat the chicken in flour, shaking off the excess flour. Coat in the egg, allowing the excess to drip back into bowl. Lastly coat in breadcrumbs, shaking off the excess.
4. Repeat the egg and breadcrumb steps to double coat the chicken.
5. Line the slow cooker with baking paper. Arrange half the chicken onto the paper in a single layer, leaving a small space between them.
6. Cover, putting a tea towel (dish towel) under the lid, and cook on HIGH for 1 hour or until cooked through. Cook other half of chicken nuggets.

NOTE: I make my own breadcrumbs. Preheat the oven to 200°C (400°F) and line a large oven tray with baking paper. Pulse 6 slices of bread in a food processor until crumbs form (you can mix the chicken stock powder through at this point if you like). Spread out on prepared tray and bake for 5 minutes or until lightly toasted. Allow to cool before using.

It's fine to use packaged breadcrumbs if you prefer.

Karen Stuckings

Wagon Wheel Cups

I came up with this idea during a week when money was short and the kids were whinging for 'something yummy' to snack on. So I rummaged through the pantry and came up with a few ingredients. After having a bit of a think about what I could make with them – Wagon Wheel Cups it was. These were a huge hit with the kids and are now always in the pantry as snacks. 10 points for this mum!

Makes 16 • Preparation 15 mins • Cook 1¼ hours • Cooker capacity 6.5 litres

170 g (6 oz) packet biscuit base mix
16 marshmallows
1 cup strawberry jam
200 g (7 oz) chocolate, melted

1. Make up the biscuit base according to the packet directions and press into a silicon patty pan tray. Place into the slow cooker.
2. Cover, putting a tea towel (dish towel) under the lid, and cook on HIGH for 1 hour.
3. Spread the bases with dollops of strawberry jam. Cut each marshmallow into 3 pieces and cover the jam. Cook for a further 15 minutes.
4. Put into the fridge to cool. Dips top into melted chocolate and leave to set.

NOTE: You'll need butter for the biscuit base – check the packet for quantity.

Faith Bennett

Wagon Wheels

This great recipe was passed from my grandmother to my mum, then to me and now my daughter, who loves to get her little hands in, especially with the dough. It's super tasty and budget friendly and the kids always go back for seconds.

Serves 6 • Preparation 15 mins • Cook 3–4 hours • Cooker capacity 6 litres

Spray oil
1½ cups self-raising flour
¾ cup milk
500 g (1 lb 2 oz) minced (ground) beef
1 small onion, finely chopped
1 tablespoon dried mixed herbs (or finely chopped fresh parsley)
2 cups grated tasty cheese
420 g (15 oz) can condensed tomato soup
Salad or veggies, to serve (or oven chips for an extra special treat)

1. Spray the inside of the slow cooker with oil. Sift the flour into a large mixing bowl and make a well in the centre. Add the milk and mix to a soft dough.
2. Roll the dough out on a lightly floured surface to a rectangle 1 cm (½ inch) thick. Spread the mince, onion, herbs and 1½ cups of the cheese over the dough.
3. Roll up the dough (like a giant sushi) to enclose the filling and cut into slices 2 cm (¾ inch) thick. Lay on the cut side in the slow cooker. Mix the soup and ½ can water in a jug and pour over the dough rounds. Sprinkle remaining cheese on top.
4. Cover and cook on HIGH for 3–4 hours, until cooked through.

NOTE: I add different veggies occasionally; it always works well. Baby spinach, grated carrot, grated zucchini or chopped mushrooms are great for extra hidden veggies!

Carly Lanigan

Coloured Bread

Serves 6 • Preparation 20 mins • Cook 1½–2 hours • Cooker capacity 6.5 litres

3 cups self-raising flour
100 g (3½ oz) butter, chopped
1 cup milk
Food colouring (4 colours)

1. Place the flour and a pinch of salt into a mixing bowl and add the butter. Use your fingertips to rub together until combined. Divide evenly into four portions.
2. Divide the milk into 4 equal portions and tint with food colouring. Working one at a time, add a portion of milk to a portion of flour and mix until evenly moistened. Gather the dough into a ball and knead gently and briefly until smooth. Repeat with remaining 3 portions of ingredients.
3. Roll out each portion of dough, then layer on top of each other. Roll together to make a long loaf. Put into a greased loaf tin.
4. Place in the slow cooker. Cover, with a tea towel (dish towel) under the lid, and cook on HIGH for 1½–2 hours, until cooked through.

Faith Bennett

Puff Pastry Ham & Cheese Scrolls

Every parent knows how hectic it is just before school goes back, so here is a simple recipe to help with the school lunches. You can add anything you like to the filling.

Serves 4–7 • Preparation 10 mins • Cook 1½ hours • Cooker capacity 5 litres

- 2 sheets frozen puff pastry, thawed
- 2 tablespoons tomato paste (concentrated purée)
- 8 slices ham
- 2 cups grated tasty cheese

1. Line the slow cooker with baking paper. Cover and preheat on HIGH.
2. Lay out the pastry sheets and spread evenly with tomato paste. Sprinkle with grated cheese and arrange the ham on top in an even layer.
3. Roll up the pastry and cut into 2.5 cm (1 inch) slices. Place into the slow cooker, spreading out so they aren't touching each other.
4. Cover, putting a tea towel (dish towel) under the lid, and cook on HIGH for 1½ hours.

Lisa Casey

Easymite scrolls

These fluffy puff pastry scrolls have a delicious Vegemite and cheese filling! I use ready-made pastry for less fuss, less mess and a tasty result guaranteed. The kids will love helping you make them too! Use an inexpensive supermarket brand pastry – you don't have to spend a lot to enjoy these treats.

Makes 18 • Preparation 20 mins • Cook 1½ hours • Cooker capacity 7 litres

Spray oil
2 sheets frozen puff pastry, just thawed
⅓ cup Vegemite
2 cups grated tasty cheese

1. Line the bottom of the slow cooker with baking paper and give a light spray of oil.
2. Lay pastry out on the work bench. Spread each sheet with Vegemite and sprinkle with cheese.
3. Roll pastry sheets up into fairly tight logs. Use a sharp knife to cut the logs into 9 slices each. Arrange cut side down in a single layer in the slow cooker.
4. Cover, putting a tea towel (dish towel) under the lid, and cook on HIGH for 1 hour. Turn scrolls over, cover (replace tea towel) and cook for a further 30 minutes.

NOTE: The 7 litre slow cooker has quite a large surface area. Depending on the size of your cooker you may need to halve the recipe, or cook in 2 batches.

Paulene Christie

Steph's Beenie Weenies

I came up with this recipe on a cold and rainy day. I wanted something filling and kid friendly. Turned out this was a winner!!

Makes 6 • Preparation 5 mins • Cook 3 hours • Cooker capacity 5 litres

2 x 400 g (14 oz) cans cannellini beans, rinsed and drained
1 teaspoon minced garlic
500 g (1 lb 2 oz) mini hotdog frankfurters, cut in half
500 ml (17 fl oz) BBQ sauce of your liking
1 onion, finely chopped
Handful of chopped parsley
Salad and crusty bread, to serve

1. Place the cannellini beans and garlic into the slow cooker and season with salt and pepper. Add the frankfurters and BBQ sauce and mix well. Stir in onion then parsley.
2. Cover and cook on HIGH for 3 hours, stirring once or twice.

Stephanie Watson

FUSSY EATERS

FUSSY EATERS

Hidden Veg Lasagne

Everyone loves lasagne, but not everyone loves to eat their vegetables. Let's hide them and see if they can find them!

Serves 6 • Preparation 20 mins • Cook 4 hours • Cooker capacity 6.5 litres

500 g (1 lb 2 oz) lean minced (ground) beef
1 zucchini, grated
1 carrot, grated
6 mushrooms, diced
4 tablespoons tomato paste (concentrated purée)
1½ tablespoons garlic paste
1 tablespoon basil paste
2 x 400 g (14 oz) cans tomato soup
Spray olive oil
5 fresh lasagne sheets
Grated cheese (I use a mixture of parmesan & low fat cheddar)

1. Lightly brown the mince in a large frying pan, breaking up lumps with a wooden spoon as it cooks. Add the zucchini, carrot and mushrooms, and the tomato, garlic and basil pastes. Combine well.
2. Stir in 1½ cans of tomato soup, then remove from the heat (the mixture should be runny).
3. Spray inside the slow cooker with olive oil and spread the remaining tomato soup over the base. Place 1 lasagne sheet in the base and cover with a third of the mince mixture. Cover with another lasagne sheet and half the remaining mince mixture. Make a double layer using 2 lasagne sheets, and spread with remaining mince mixture. Top with the last lasagne sheet.
4. Cover and cook on LOW for 2 hours. Sprinkle lasagne with cheese (as much or as little as you like). Cover and cook on LOW for a further 2 hours.

NOTE: You'll find garlic paste and basil paste in tubes in the fruit and veggie section of the supermarket.

Denise Roberts

Sausage Ragout

I came up with this recipe a couple of years ago for a 'cooking for kids' challenge as a twist on our usual sausages and gravy. This also works well as a handy dump bag in the freezer.

Serves 4 • Preparation 5 mins • Cook 4–5 hours • Cooker capacity 5.5 litres

10 beef sausages, cut in half
1 red onion, sliced
500 g (1 lb 2 oz) mushrooms, sliced
⅓ cup gravy powder
250 ml (9 fl oz) beef or vegetable stock
400 g (14 oz) tomatoes, chopped
3–4 garlic cloves, finely chopped
½ teaspoon chopped fresh rosemary
Pinch cracked pepper

1. Place sausages into the slow cooker and scatter the onion and mushrooms over.
2. Whisk the gravy powder and stock in a large jug or a bowl. Add the tomatoes, garlic and rosemary, and season with black pepper. Pour over sausages.
3. Cover and cook on LOW for 4–5 hours.

Felicity Barnett

Lydia's Minestrone Alphabet Soup

This recipe is dedicated to my Nan who always used to make this for us as kids. It was my favourite and she always made sure we had it every time I visited.

Serves 8 • Preparation 5 mins • Cook 2½ hours • Cooker capacity 3 litres

- 4 cups salt-reduced chicken stock
- 400 g (14 oz) can diced tomatoes with herbs
- 1 tablespoon tomato paste (concentrated purée)
- 1 onion, cut into large pieces
- 1 celery stalk, cut into large pieces
- 2 tablespoons roughly chopped parsley
- 1 teaspoon chopped oregano,
- 1 garlic clove, bruised with a knife
- ⅓ cup small soup pasta, alphabet if possible!
- Parmesan cheese, to serve

1. Place the stock, tomatoes and tomato paste into the slow cooker and season with pepper. Stir in the onion, celery, parsley, oregano and garlic.
2. Cover and cook on HIGH for 2 hours.
3. Use a slotted spoon to remove the vegetables. Add the pasta and cook for a further 30 minutes or until tender. Serve topped with freshly shaved parmesan.

NOTE: If your kids aren't too fussy, chop the veggies smaller and leave in. You could add more too!

Kelly Joyce

Dad's Beef Curry

This recipe has been a favourite at family functions for years. It was created by my late father David, but converted to the slow cooker by me. The recipe has a beautiful sweetness to it that lessens the heat of the curry powder, making it suitable for children to eat. At a recent family function there were no seconds to be had because the grandchildren had demolished it.

Serves about 12 (with rice) • Preparation 15–20 minutes
Cook 6–8 hours • Cooker capacity 6 litres

- 2 kg (4 lb 6 oz) diced beef
- 2 onions, diced
- 1 tablespoon oil (optional)
- 4 tablespoons curry powder
- 2 cups diced carrots
- 1 cup diced celery
- 1 cup sultanas
- 1¼ cups plum jam
- 440 g (15½ oz) can crushed pineapple
- 2 teaspoons beef stock powder
- 1 tablespoon butter
- 1 tablespoon plain (all-purpose) flour

1. If you like, brown the beef and onion in the oil in a frying pan, adding the curry powder towards the end of browning. Otherwise, place straight into the slow cooker with the vegetables, sultanas, jam, pineapple and stock powder. Fill the empty can with water, swish around and add to slow cooker.
2. Cover and cook on LOW for 6–8 hours.
3. When the curry is almost ready, melt the butter in a small saucepan over medium heat and add the flour. Stir for a minute or two to cook the flour. Stir into the curry and cook a little longer until thickened.

NOTE: Add turnip or swede if desired. You can melt the plum jam in a microwave before adding to slow cooker. Add as much or as little curry as suited to your taste.

Kathryn Ryles

Big Mac Chicken

This dish came about after trialling home-made Big Mac-style sauces for burgers at home. However, my fussy toddler was in a pasta-only stage so I put our leftovers on some penne. I realised it tasted pretty good and the recipe developed from there!

Serves 4 (adult serves) • Preparation 15 mins • Cook 3 hours • Cooker capacity 6 litres

500 g (1 lb 2 oz) chicken breast, diced
1 large onion, sliced
1 cup mayonnaise
2 tablespoons sweet mustard pickles
2 tablespoons French dressing
1 tablespoon Thousand Island dressing
2 teaspoons vinegar
1 teaspoon sugar
Pinch salt
Squirt tomato sauce
Sliced dill pickle, to serve
Pasta, to serve

1. Brown the chicken in a frying pan. Combine in the slow cooker with the remaining ingredients (except the dill pickle) and ¼ cup water.
2. Cover and cook on LOW for 3 hours.
3. Stir through sliced pickle and serve on pasta.

NOTE: This would be great with lettuce for burgers or wraps, or with rice too!

Eliza Ramskill

Creamy Cheesy Chicken & Pasta

I love this dish – so simple, so quick to prepare and the whole family love it! I'd been trying to get into eating pasta but had never found anything I liked it with – until now. This is one of our midweek favourites.

Serves 4 • Preparation 10 mins • Cook 4–5 hours • Cooker capacity 4.5 litres

- 500 g (1 lb 2 oz) diced chicken
- 420 g (15 oz) can condensed cream of chicken soup
- 20 g (¾ oz) cheese sauce mix
- ½ teaspoon dried parsley
- 250–300 g (9–10½ oz) pasta (any kind)
- 100 g (3½ oz) grated tasty cheese

1. Place the diced chicken in an even layer in the bottom of the slow cooker. Season well with salt and pepper.
2. Mix the chicken soup with the cheese sauce mix and add the parsley. Pour over the chicken, as evenly as possible.
3. Cover and cook on LOW for 3–4 hours. Stir in the pasta and grated cheese. Cover and cook for a further 1 hour, until the pasta is tender.

NOTE: For extra flavour why not add some bacon bits and onion.

Rachel Duncan

Family Friendly Beef Curry

Our family loves a good curry, but with children ranging in age from 14 down to 4, I need to keep the heat out of the curry so we can all enjoy the same meal. This is a slow cooked, coconut cream based mild, meaty curry. You'll be sure to want seconds!

Serves 5 • Preparation 15 mins • Cook 7 hours • Cooker capacity 6 litres

- 1 kg (2 lb 3 oz) blade steak, cubed
- 1 large onion, diced
- 400 ml (13½ fl oz) can coconut cream
- 1 tablespoon minced garlic
- 1 tablespoon soy sauce
- 1 tablespoon brown sugar
- 3 teaspoons mild curry powder
- 2 teaspoons minced ginger
- 2 teaspoons cornflour (cornstarch)
- ½ teaspoon ground turmeric
- 1–2 tablespoons cornflour (cornstarch), extra

1. Place the beef and onion into the slow cooker. Combine all other ingredients (except the extra cornflour), and pour over the beef and onion.
2. Cover and cook on LOW for 7 hours. In the last 30 minutes of cooking, mix the extra cornflour and 2 tablespoons water in a small bowl until smooth. Stir into the sauce and finish cooking.

NOTE: If you like a hotter curry, add more curry powder. The cooking time will easily stretch to 8 hours if that works for you.

Paulene Christie

Creamy Chicken Delight

This is a quick and easy chicken dish your kids will demolish!

Serves 6 • Preparation 15 mins • Cook 4–5 hours • Cooker capacity 6 litres

1 tablespoon oil
5 chicken thigh fillets
8 rashers bacon, chopped
250 g mushrooms, sliced
1 tablespoon minced garlic
150 g sundried tomatoes, chopped
1 cup cream
¼ cup chicken stock
Sprinkle dried Italian herbs
Pasta, rice or mash, to serve
Parmesan, pine nuts and spinach, to serve (optional)

1. Heat oil in a frying pan and brown the chicken. Set aside. Add the bacon, mushrooms and garlic to the frying pan and cook until mushrooms soften.
2. Add bacon mixture to the slow cooker along with the sundried tomatoes, cream and stock. Add a sprinkle of herbs and stir to combine. Add the chicken. Season with salt and pepper.
3. Cover and cook on LOW for 4–5 hours.
4. Remove the chicken and shred the meat. Stir back into the sauce. Serve on pasta, rice or mash with parmesan, pine nuts and spinach leaves if desired.

Stella Thomson

Chicken, Chorizo & Vegetable One-Pot Dinner

Even my fussiest eater devours this quick, easy and tasty little dish.

Serves 5 • Preparation 15 mins • Cook 6 hours • Cooker capacity 4.5 litres

1 kg (2 lb 3 oz) baby new potatoes, halved
5 chicken breast fillets
150 g (5½ oz) chorizo, sliced
2 garlic cloves, finely chopped
400 g (14 oz) jar passata (puréed tomatoes)
1 teaspoon paprika
Chopped veggies of your choice (see note)

1. Place the potatoes into the slow cooker and place chicken on top. Sprinkle with chorizo, then the garlic.
2. Mix the passata and paprika in a jug and season with salt and pepper. Pour over everything in the slow cooker. Add any vegetables you want.
3. Cover and cook on LOW for 6 hours.

NOTE: I add some cherry tomatoes, two quartered onions, sweet corn and sliced zucchini (courgette). I leave them chunky so my eldest can avoid them (but I hide blitzed veggies in the passata – shhh). If you have lots of fussy eaters and want to leave out the veggies, this is great served with roasted vegetables as a side dish.

Stephanie Brookes

BBQ Chicken Drumsticks

This is a nice easy dish to prepare – my 11 year old likes to make it! Easy and flavoursome, and the meat falls off the bone when done.

Serves 7–8 • Preparation 5 mins • Cook 5–6 hours • Cooker capacity 5.5 litres

2 kg (4 lb 6 oz) chicken drumsticks
1 onion, sliced
⅔ cup BBQ sauce
¼ cup soy sauce
¼ cup brown sugar
2 garlic cloves, minced
Steamed rice, to serve

1. Place the chicken drumsticks into the slow cooker. Add the onion.
2. Mix the other ingredients together and pour over the chicken.
3. Cover and cook on LOW for 5–6 hours.
4. When cooked, take the chicken meat off the bones. Serve over rice, with the sauce spooned over the top.

Lynda Eagleson

Easy Chicken & Pasta

This is so easy to prepare and the kids absolutely love it.

Serves 4 • Preparation 10 mins • Cook 6–8 hours • Cooker capacity 6 litres

500 g (1 lb 2 oz) chicken fillets (breast or thigh), cut into pieces
420 g (15 oz) can condensed cream of chicken soup
Pasta, to serve

1. Brown the chicken in a frying pan then transfer to the slow cooker. Add the soup and a can of water.
2. Cover and cook on LOW for 6–8 hours. Serve over pasta.

NOTE: You could serve over rice instead of pasta if you like.

Kim O'Grady

Chicken Fiesta

This came about because I couldn't be bothered to go shopping and used what I had on hand. It's simple and can be changed to suit your family. It can be served on rice or in tortillas or wraps, or just with corn chips.

Serves 4 • Preparation 10 mins • Cook 4 hours • Cooker capacity 3 litres

- 500 g (1 lb 2 oz) chicken breast fillets, cubed
- 2 x 300 g (10½ oz) jars salsa
- 400 g (14 oz) can cannellini beans, rinsed and drained (optional, or use beans of your choice)
- 1 cup corn kernels
- 1 red capsicum (pepper), chopped (optional)
- Grated cheese, sliced avocado and sour cream, to serve

1. Place the chicken, salsa, beans, corn and capsicum into the slow cooker.
2. Cover and cook on LOW for 4 hours.
3. Serve sprinkled with grated cheese, topped with avocado and sour cream.

NOTE: Chopped celery would also be a nice addition.

Karen Stuckings

SLOW COOKER IN A HURRY

Chocolate Bread & Butter Pudding

Bread and butter pudding is my all time favourite dessert. My children hate raisins (and gone are the days I can eat a whole pudding to myself!) so together we whipped up this version for the whole family to enjoy.

Serves 6 • Preparation 15 mins • Cook 2 hours • Cooker capacity 4.5 litres

- 10–12 slices white bread, crusts cut off
- 75 g (2½ oz) soft butter
- 100 g (3½ oz) chocolate spread
- ⅓ cup caster sugar
- ½ cup chocolate chips (or raisins or banana slices)
- 4 eggs
- 2¼ cups milk
- Ice-cream, cream or custard, to serve

1. Grease the inside of the slow cooker or line with baking paper. Spread the slices of bread with butter, then chocolate spread. Cut the bread slices in half (we like triangles).
2. Line the bottom of the slow cooker with one layer of bread slices, chocolate side up. Sprinkle a third of the caster sugar and half of the chocolate chips on top.
3. Repeat with a layer of bread slices, then the rest of the chocolate chips and another third of the caster sugar over them. Add a final layer of bread and sprinkle with the remaining caster sugar.
4. Whisk the eggs and mix together. Pour the milk mixture over the layers in the slow cooker, trying to get in all the gaps and corners.
5. Cover and cook on HIGH for two hours.
6. Serve hot or cold with ice cream, cream or custard.

Stephanie Brookes

Caz's 3 C's Dish

The kids will love to eat this as well as make it. It is a very quick, easy and cheap meal. The title is from the three ingredients starting with C… and of course I say CC!

Serves 4–6 • Preparation 20 mins • Cook 1 hour 15 mins • Cooker capacity 5 litres

400 g (14 oz) can diced tomatoes
1 kg (2 lb 3 oz) small frankfurts, sliced into pieces
2 cups grated pizza cheese
175 g packet corn chips

1. Pour the tomatoes into the slow cooker, then stir in the frankfurts.
2. Cover, putting a tea towel (dish towel) under the lid, and cook on HIGH for 1 hour.
3. Sprinkle the cheese over the top and cook a bit longer until almost melted.
4. To serve, prod half the corn chips into the mixture, and serve with the other half for dipping.

NOTE: This dish is yummy for the adults as well. You could replace the frankfurts with kabana or chorizo and add some capsicum as well.

Carol Wilkinson

Sweet Chilli Sausages & Beans

My boys love helping make this for lunch on the weekends. It's also great as a filling snack before sports training during the week.

Serves 6 • Preparation 5 mins • Cook 2 hours • Cooker capacity 6 litres

380 g (13 oz) jar German-style skinless cocktail franks
2 x 425 g (15 oz) cans baked beans (I prefer the ones in ham sauce)
2 x 400 g (14 oz) cans borlotti beans, rinsed and drained
¼ cup sweet chilli sauce
¼ cup brown sugar
1 tablespoon Worcestershire sauce
Buttered toast, to serve

1. Place the franks and beans into the slow cooker. Mix all the other ingredients together and stir in.
2. Cover and cook on HIGH for 2 hours.
3. Serve with buttered toast.

Fiona Masters

Tuna, Mac & Cheese

This is a lovely quick family meal.

Serves 4 • Preparation 5 mins • Cook 2 hours • Cooker capacity 6.5 litres

¼ cup plain (all-purpose) flour
1 garlic clove, minced
4 cups reduced-fat milk
250 g (9 oz) macaroni pasta
1 cup frozen peas or corn
425 g (15 oz) can tuna in spring water, drained & flaked
1½ cups grated low-fat cheddar cheese

1. Place the flour and garlic into the slow cooker and gradually add the milk, whisking until smooth. Stir in the macaroni and peas or corn.
2. Cover and cook on LOW for 1 hour, stirring occasionally. Stir in the tuna and 1 cup of the cheese. Sprinkle the remaining cheese over the top and continue to cook for 1 more hour.

NOTE: You could replace tuna with diced bacon, and add diced celery instead of peas or corn.

Denise Roberts

Chilli Kicker Chicken

This is an easy, budget-friendly pulled chicken. Keep the sweet chilli sauce mild enough for your children's tastes and everyone can enjoy it. This recipe is easy enough for your kids to help you cook too!

Serves 6–8 • Preparation 5 mins • Cook 5½ hours • Cooker capacity 6 litres

2 kg (4 lb 6 oz) chicken drumsticks (about 16)
2 large onions, sliced
40 g (1½ oz) packet French onion soup mix
½ cup mild sweet chilli sauce
Vegetables and rice or mash, to serve

1. Place the chicken drumsticks and onions into the slow cooker. Sprinkle the soup mix over the chicken. Pour the sauce over the top, spreading it around as much as you can as you pour it.
2. Cover and cook on LOW for about 5 hours.
3. Remove chicken from the cooker, and strip the meat from the bones. Discard the bones and return the meat to the cooker. Cook for a further 30 minutes.

NOTE: This makes a lot so we often freeze half to use for another meal.

Paulene Christie

Satay Wings

I think the term 'finger licking good' was created for wing recipes like these – so good! Delicious with your favourite sides or on their own. No extra sauce needed for these tasty morsels!

Serves 2 as a main or 4 as a side dish • Preparation 10 mins
Cook 2 or 3–4 hours • Cooker capacity 6 litres

500 g (1 lb 2 oz) chicken wings
¼ cup peanut butter
1 tablespoon tomato sauce (ketchup)
1 tablespoon salt-reduced soy sauce

1. Place the wings into a large bowl. Add all the other ingredients and stir to coat well. Transfer to the slow cooker.
2. Cover, putting a tea towel (dish towel) under the lid, and cook on HIGH for 2 hours or LOW for 3–4 hours.

NOTE: I like the chicken wings cut into sections, with the tips removed, but it's up to you. Season with salt and pepper if you like.

Paulene Christie

Gooey Rice Bubble Bars

This is a recipe that I was taught as a child, making it on the stove. I was easily able to alter it to suit a slow cooker and teach my son. I love that it is a bit messy, which is fun for kids. It's really easy to make, and super yummy to eat afterwards! We like to make these for birthdays or holidays, and even just when our sweet tooth is acting up.

Makes 12–24 bars • Preparation 15 mins • Cook 15 mins
Cooker capacity 5.5 litres (or larger)

- 60 g butter, chopped
- 4¼ cups mini marshmallows
- 6 cups puffed rice cereal
- Spray oil
- Toppings (such as sprinkles, choc chips, candies)

1. Preheat the slow cooker on HIGH. Add the butter and leave to melt. Add the marshmallows, cover and leave for about 5 minutes, to melt. Stir well, and let melt for another 1–2 minutes. Stir again, until smooth.
2. Add the puffed rice cereal, and stir gently until coated evenly with the marshmallow mixture. Spray a 33 x 23 cm (13 x 9 inch) slice pan with oil. Pour the mixture into the pan.
3. Lightly spray your hands with oil and press the mixture into the pan, getting into the corners. Cover with sprinkles, choc chips or candies to decorate. Leave to set, then cut into bars or squares to serve.

NOTE: Use cookie cutters to cut out shapes if you like, and you can tint the mixture with food colouring to suit. Try Christmas trees, pumpkins for Halloween, or egg shapes for Easter!

Melissa Hansen

Sweet Apple Sultana Damper

I wanted something easy, tasty and with no added sugar, so I tried this and loved it.

Makes 8 slices • Preparation 5 mins • Cook 1½ hours • Cooker capacity 3.5 litre

- 3 cups self-raising flour
- 1 cup sultanas
- ¾ cup Splenda (sugar substitute)
- 500 ml (17 fl oz) apple juice

1. Sift the flour into a mixing bowl and stir in the sultanas and Splenda. Make a well in the centre.
2. Add the apple juice and mix until just combined. Grease the slow cooker or line with baking paper.
3. Cover, putting a tea towel (dish towel) under the lid, and cook on HIGH for 1½ hours. Insert a knife into the centre of damper and remove it. If the knife comes out clean, the damper is ready. If the knife comes out doughy, cook for a further 10 minutes and repeat the knife test. If necessary, repeat extra cooking time and knife test until the damper is cooked through.
4. Tip the damper onto a cooling rack.

NOTE: Best served hot and fresh with melted butter, and honey if you like it.

Darren Comley

Savoury Cheese Spread

This is such a versatile recipe as it can be used for many things. We often make cheese rolls (see note) as they are a favourite in my part of the world.

Serves many! • Preparation 10 mins • Cook 1 hour 10 mins • Cooker capacity 3 litre

- 1 kg (2 lb 3 oz) grated tasty cheese
- 2 x 40 g (1½ oz) packets French onion soup mix
- 1–2 teaspoons mustard powder (optional)
- 2 x 375 ml (12 ½ fl oz) cans evaporated milk (or fresh milk, or half fresh, half evaporated)
- Optional add-ins: finely chopped onion, bacon and/or parsley, canned corn kernels or creamed corn, canned crushed pineapple. If adding crushed pineapple or creamed corn, omit about ⅓ cup milk per can of these.

1. Place everything into the slow cooker.
2. Cover and cook on HIGH for about 1 hour, stirring every 20 minutes, until cheese has melted. Remove lid and cook for a further 10 minutes.
3. Turn off slow cooker and leave to cool for a while so that the mixture thickens to an easily spreadable yet still quite liquid consistency. Stir occasionally as the fat content of the cheese will try to separate out.

NOTE: Use cheese spread to make grilled cheese (spread onto toast and grilled) or as a topping on a baked potato. For a quick and easy cheese sauce, just thin with milk. The cheese spread (made without any of the add-ins) will keep in the fridge for 1–2 weeks.

To make Cheese rolls, cut crusts from sliced white bread (keep crusts to make breadcrumbs). Spread bread with a thin layer of the cheese spread, and roll up. Place in a sandwich press or under the grill until browned on both sides and cheese melted. You can spread a little butter on one side but it's not necessary.

Nikki Willis

Cheesy Baked Bean Pasties

I admit it ... I'm a baked beans kid! I've lived on a diet high in baked beans my entire life – I love, love, love beans and so do my kids. Nothing says 'easy dinner' like beans on toast, and this is the slightly more upmarket sister dish – cheesy bean pasties.

Makes 4 • Preparation 20 mins • Cook 1 hour 20 mins • Cooker capacity 6 litres

½ cup grated tasty cheese
¼ cup grated mozzarella cheese
200 g (7 oz) can baked beans
1 sheet frozen puff pastry, just thawed
1 egg, lightly beaten

1. Line the bottom of the slow cooker with baking paper and give a light spray of oil.
2. Combine the two grated cheeses together in a bowl. Remove the excess sauce from the baked beans and discard.
3. Cut pastry into 4 squares. Place a triangle area of cheese into one half of each square. Add about 2 tablespoons of baked beans to each cheese area. Fold the other half of each pastry square over the beans and cheese to form a triangle-shaped pastie. Press the join with a fork to seal.
4. Arrange the pasties in a single layer in the slow cooker, and lightly brush top of each one with the egg.
5. Cover, putting a tea towel (dish towel) under the lid, and cook on HIGH for 40 minutes. Turn pasties over and brush the other side with egg. Cover (replace tea towel) and cook for a further 40 minutes.

NOTE: Serve these hot and fresh, or cool and wrap in foil for lunchboxes.

Paulene Christie

French Cream Chicken – 4 Ingredients!

An ahhhh-mazing tasting creamy chicken dish. I created this when I wanted something to suit my low carb life but that the whole family could enjoy with me. You can vary the flavour of the cream cheese you use in this dish to vary the flavour of the end result (see alternative versions below). It's also a great way to get your kids to eat more spinach for its exceptionally high nutritional value without really noticing. Since I first cooked this recipe it has now become a weekly regular in our house, we love it that much!

Serves 2 • Preparation 15 mins • Cook 1 hour 20 mins • Cooker capacity 6 litres

500 g (1 lb 2 oz) chicken thigh fillets, diced
110 g (3¾ oz) block French onion cream cheese (or other flavour – see note)
200 ml (6¾ fl oz) cooking cream
60 g (2 oz) baby spinach leaves

1. Brown the chicken in a searing slow cooker (or frying pan, then transfer to the slow cooker). Add the cream cheese and stir for 2–3 minutes to melt and coat the chicken. Stir in the cooking cream.
2. Cover, putting a tea towel (dish towel) under the lid, and cook on HIGH for 1 hour 15 minutes.
3. Add the spinach and stir until wilted before serving.

NOTE: If you cannot source the French onion flavoured cream cheese you could use regular cream cheese and mix with 20 g (¾ oz) dry French onion soup mix. Try also sweet chilli cream cheese, chive and onion, or apricot. I've also replaced the baby spinach with semidried tomatoes for another yummy version. The cooking cream is important as it resists splitting like normal cream. This recipe can be doubled to feed a larger crowd. Doing so won't affect the cooking time by much; about 15 minutes extra will be all that's needed at most.

Paulene Christie

Mexican Baguette

A cheesy taco-filled baguette – this is great for entertaining or kids to enjoy (easy for your children to help you make them too). It is also great as a flavour-packed side dish at your next Mexican feast!

Makes 1 baguette • Preparation 20 mins • Cook 1¼ hours • Cooker capacity 6 litres

1 baguette (French bread stick), about 30 cm (12 inches) long
½ cup nachos sauce
1 cup leftover cooked Taco Mince (see Simple Taco Mince, page 111)
1–1½ cups grated tasty cheese

1. Cut the baguette into slices about 2.5 cm (1 inch) wide, without cutting all the way through (like garlic bread would be sliced).
2. Tear a strip of aluminium foil a little longer than the baguette. Place the baguette onto the foil. Place about 1 teaspoon of nachos sauce into each cut, reserving 2 tablespoons for top of finished baguette. Add a small sprinkle of cheese into each cut.
3. Spoon Taco Mince into the cuts, dividing evenly. Top with another sprinkle of cheese. Push all together to close the cuts and reshape the baguette as much as possible.
4. Spread the reserved 2 tablespoons of nachos sauce along the top of the baguette and sprinkle with any remaining grated cheese. Wrap the baguette in foil and seal. Place into the slow cooker.
5. Cover and cook and cook on HIGH for about 1¼ hours or until the cheese has melted and the baguette has heated through. Serve immediately – or prepare ahead of time and cook just in time to serve for a great party food!

Paulene Christie

Cheese & Bacon Croissants

I felt like making bacon and cheese bread but didn't want the effort of making the dough. I had some stale croissants in the fridge and so my recipe was created.

Serves 4 • Preparation 5 mins • Cook 1¾ hours • Cooker capacity 3.5 litres

6 small croissants, halved or cut to fit
4 eggs
¼ cup milk
1 teaspoon vegetable stock powder
¼ teaspoon onion powder
¼ teaspoon garlic powder
½ cup grated tasty cheese
½ cup diced bacon

1. Layer the croissants in the bottom of a slice pan that will fit into the slow cooker.
2. Whisk the eggs, milk, stock powder, onion powder and garlic powder in a jug. Pour over the croissants. Sprinkle the cheese and bacon over the top.
3. Pour about 1 cup hot water into the slow cooker and place the pan in it (water should come about halfway up sides of pan).
4. Cover, putting a tea towel (dish towel) under the lid, and cook on HIGH for 1¾ hours or until the cheese has melted and the egg is cooked.

NOTE: I used 4 eggs because I only used a small tray, but you could definitely use more.

Erin Ilalio

Poached Asian Chicken

This is a versatile, flavourful, poached chicken fillet to use in one of many meals of your choice. Serve whole, sliced or shredded depending on how you wish to use it. Great for kids' lunchbox sandwiches, salads, pizza toppers, wraps, as a main course with veg or salad or any way you can think of!

Serves 4 • Preparation 5 mins • Cook 1½ hours • Cooker capacity 5 litres

- 2 chicken breast fillets (or 4 thigh fillets)
- 2 cups chicken stock
- 1 tablespoon reduced-salt soy sauce
- 2 teaspoons minced garlic
- 2 teaspoons sesame oil
- 1 heaped teaspoon minced ginger

1. Place the chicken fillets into the slow cooker. Combine all the other ingredients and pour over, then season with sea salt and cracked black pepper.
2. Cook on HIGH for 1 hour 30 mins or until cooked through. I turn mine over halfway through cooking.
3. Remove chicken from cooking liquid and serve whole or shred to use as desired.

NOTE: You can easily increase the amount of chicken you use and still have enough liquid. Just ensure chicken is mostly covered and flip it halfway to get colour on both sides.

Paulene Christie

Easy Peasy Cheesy Rolls

This is a simple enough recipe the kids can do with minimal supervision, or you can throw it together quickly for an eat and run breakfast or dinner.

Makes 12 rolls • Preparation 5 mins • Cook 1½ hours • Cooker capacity 7 litres

12 bread rolls
Approximately 500 g grated cheese (we used a mix of regular block and provolone)
Fillings of choice, such as sliced ham, sliced roast beef, pineapple slices, sliced tomatoes, onions or mushrooms.

1. Slice rolls in half and place bases into the slow cooker. Sprinkle with some grated cheese.
2. Layer with your fillings of choice and sprinkle with more cheese. Place top half of rolls over the fillings.
3. Cover, putting a tea towel (dish towel) under the lid, and cook on HIGH for about 90 minutes, until the cheese is melted and gooey.

Felicity Barnett

EVERYDAY CROWDPLEASERS

EVERYDAY
CROWDPLEASERS

Simple Taco Mince

Kids love tacos! Ours love to assemble their own tacos, so why not involve them in the cooking stage also. We wanted to include this recipe to show that making regular Mexican mince in your slow cooker is totally possible, and easy as. Whether you like to blend your own spices or use a packet mix, this is a SUPER SIMPLE way to cook it. This is the only way we make ours now.

Serves 5 • Preparation 5 mins • Cook 3–4 hours • Cooker capacity 6 litres

1 kg (2 lb 3 oz) minced (ground) beef, chicken or pork
40 g (1½ oz) packet taco seasoning

1. Place the mince and seasoning into the slow cooker and add ½ cup water. I add my mince raw but you could brown it first if you wish to.
2. Cover and cook on low for 3–4 hours.

NOTE: Serve in your favourite Mexican meal, such as tacos, taco salads, wraps, or even on pizza. You can also make your taco seasoning mix from scratch if you prefer. My recipe for this is in *Slow Cooker Central 2* and on our website.

Paulene Christie

Creamy Vegetable Curry

I love this recipe because it's a great mild curry introduction for the kids. It's a fantastic way to get some extra vegetables into them and a lovely creamy (but not rich) meat-free alternative. We love it with rice and pappadums for an easy weekend meal!

Serves 2 adults + 3 kids and maybe a small lunch • Preparation 15–20 mins • Cook 3–3½ hours • Cooker capacity 4.5 litres

1 onion, cut into wedges
2 carrots, chopped
2 cups cubed pumpkin
½ small cauliflower, cut into florets
2 teaspoons curry powder
50 g (1¾ oz) packet chicken noodle soup mix
⅓ cup light sour cream
½ cup frozen peas
Steamed rice and pappadums, to serve

1. Combine the onion, carrot, pumpkin, cauliflower, curry powder, soup mix and 1 cup water in the slow cooker.
2. Cover and cook on LOW for 2½–3 hours (depending how you like your vegetables). Stir occasionally to check the tenderness of the vegetables. Add more water if the liquid has been absorbed and the vegetables are still hard.
3. Stir in the sour cream and peas, and cook a further 15–30 minutes or until the peas are cooked through. Serve with steamed rice and pappadums.

Fiona McIldowney

Tasty Tomato Beef in Gravy

A tasty tomato beef casserole in a rich gravy that's plate licking good! We like to serve ours with creamy mashed potato and steamed green vegetables.

Serves 5 • Preparation 15 mins • Cook 5 hours • Cooker capacity 6 litres

1kg (2 lb 3 oz) chuck (or other stewing) steak, diced
1 onion, diced
2 tablespoons tomato paste
1 tablespoon beef stock powder
250 g (9 oz) cherry tomatoes

1. Combine the beef, onion, tomato paste and stock powder in the slow cooker. Mix well. Add the whole cherry tomatoes on top.
2. Cover and cook on low for 4½ hours.
3. Give it a good stir to help the tomatoes break down and mix with the meat. Cook for a further 30 minutes, then serve.

Paulene Christie

Naked Chicken Parmigiana

Super easy, super tasty… naked parmigiana! It's just like regular parmi but without the crumbs, and still all the cheesy tomato goodness you expect! Serve with chips and salad or veggies.

Serves 4 • Preparation 10 mins • Cook 4¼ hours • Cooker capacity 6 litres

1 kg (2 lb 3 oz) chicken thigh fillets
500 g (1 lb 2 oz) bottle napoletana or parmigiana sauce (see note)
200 g (7 oz) grated mozzarella cheese

1. Place the chicken into the slow cooker and pour the sauce over.
2. Cover and cook on LOW for 4 hours.
3. Sprinkle chicken with cheese. Cover, putting a tea towel (dish towel) under the lid, and cook for a further 15 minutes or until the cheese has melted.

NOTE: Use your favourite sauce – I used chunky tomato with herbs. If you prefer, before adding cheese, remove some of the excess cooking liquid by scooping it out with a large spoon.

Paulene Christie

Saucy Chicken

A tasty, budget family chicken recipe for the family. If you have kids keen to help you cook, this is a great one for letting them help measure out all the spoon measures for you. You could substitute other cuts of chicken for the drumsticks, or even use fillets if you prefer.

Serves 5 • Preparation 10 mins • Cook 4½ hours • Cooker capacity 6 litres

- 10 chicken drumsticks
- 2 tablespoons honey
- 2 tablespoons tomato sauce (ketchup)
- 2 tablespoons sweet chilli sauce
- 2 teaspoons salt-reduced soy sauce
- 2 teaspoons Worcestershire sauce
- 2 teaspoons minced garlic
- 2 teaspoons minced ginger
- 2 teaspoons sesame seeds

1. Place the chicken drumsticks into the slow cooker. Combine all the other ingredients and pour over the chicken.
2. Cover and cook on LOW for 4½ hours. If you are around during the cooking time, baste the chicken with the sauce occasionally for a richer colour.

Paulene Christie

Chicken & Gravy

This is a fast, simple, easy, budget-friendly family favourite. It's perfect for serve yourself or grab and go dinners, or any get together. It also works well as a pie filling and a handy dump bag in the freezer.

Serves 4–6 • Preparation 5–10 mins • Cook 4–5 hours • Cooker capacity 5.5 litres

1.5 kg (3 lb 5 oz) chicken thigh fillets
4 cups chicken stock (or water)
½ cup gravy powder
Mashed potato or bread rolls and salad, to serve

OPTIONAL EXTRAS
1 or 2 onions, sliced
2 garlic cloves, sliced
200 g (7 oz) mushrooms, sliced

1. Place the chicken (and any of the optional extras, if using) into the slow cooker.
2. Mix the stock (or water) and the gravy powder together, and pour over the chicken.
3. Cover and cook on LOW for 4–5 hours.
4. Serve with mashed potato or in rolls, with salad.

Felicity Barnett

Easy Budget BBQ Chicken

Fast and easy to cook, and nice and easy on the budget too! This saucy slow cooked BBQ chicken will be a hit with the whole family.

Serves 5 • Preparation 15 mins • Cook 4 hours • Cooker capacity 6 litres

1 kg (2 lb 3 oz) chicken pieces of your choice
1 large onion, sliced
1 cup BBQ sauce (I used sugar-free sauce; use regular if you prefer)
1 heaped teaspoon minced garlic
½ teaspoon smoked paprika

1. Place the chicken into the slow cooker and top with the onion. Combine all the other ingredients and pour over the chicken.
2. Cook on LOW for 4 hours. If you are around, turn chicken over once or twice during cooking.

NOTE: To prevent the finished sauce from being too watery, as I lift the lid I make sure I direct the run-off of water under the lid into the sink or onto a cloth instead of back in the cooking bowl.

Paulene Christie

Simple Sensational Pulled Beef

A simple, slow cooked, 3 ingredient pulled beef. It's so versatile – serve with salad, on wraps and pizzas or even on subs.

Serves 8+ • Preparation 10 mins • Cook 7–8 hours • Cooker capacity 6 litres

1 large onion, sliced
1.5 kg (3 lb 5 oz) stewing beef, such as chuck, gravy or oyster blade
40 g (1½ oz) sachet rib spice rub (see note)

1. Lay the onion slices on the base of the slow cooker bowl, and add the beef. Sprinkle the spice rub over and add 1 cup water.
2. Cover and cook on LOW for 7–8 hours.
3. Pull the beef into shreds (use plastic utensils so you don't damage the bowl) and mix through the sauce.

NOTE: Look in the spice section at the supermarket for spice rub mixtures.

Paulene Christie

Pulled Pork on Your Fork

Serve this pulled pork on burger buns, on pizza, or with salad or veggies. Any way you like!

Serves 8 • Preparation 15 mins • Cook 8 hours • Cooker capacity 6 litres

2 kg (4 lb 6 oz) boneless pork shoulder roast
1 large onion, cut into 8 wedges
½ cup apricot jam
¼ cup mild mustard
1 tablespoon wholegrain mustard

1. Arrange half the onion over the base of the slow cooker bowl. Remove any netting from the pork and place onto the onion, fat side down. Scatter the remaining onion around the pork.
2. Combine the mustard and jam and brush onto pork (use it all up).
3. Cover and cook on LOW for 8 hours.
4. Gently turn the pork over. Carefully remove the fat layer and discard it. Pull the meat (with plastic or silicone tools to protect your slow cooker) into shreds, and mix through the cooking juices.

Paulene Christie

Creamy Garlic Chicken Made Easy!

Serves 4 • Preparation 15 mins • Cook 2 hours • Cooker capacity 5 litres

700 g (1 lb 9 oz) skinless chicken thigh fillets, diced into small pieces
1 tablespoon minced garlic
300 ml (10 fl oz) cooking cream
1 cup grated tasty cheese, plus extra to serve

1. Sear the chicken and garlic in a searing slow cooker or on the stovetop until lightly browned.
2. Combine the chicken, garlic and cream in the slow cooker. Season to taste with salt and pepper.
3. Cover, putting a tea towel (dish towel) under the lid, and cook on LOW for 2 hours.
4. Add the cheese and stir to melt. Serve with extra cheese sprinkled on top.

NOTE: Larger chicken pieces will require extra cooking time. The cooking cream is important as it resists splitting like normal cream.

Paulene Christie

Kids' Curry

This is an easy, nutritious meal made with ingredients that are probably in your pantry right now!

Serves 6 • Preparation 15 mins • Cook 4 hours • Cooker capacity 3.5 litres

500 g (1 lb 2 oz) minced (ground) beef
440 g can pineapple pieces, including juice
1 onion, diced
1 carrot, diced
1 green apple, peeled and diced
1 zucchini, diced
½ each green and red capsicum (pepper), diced
50 g (1¾ oz) packet chicken noodle soup mix
2 teaspoons curry powder (your favourite)
2 teaspoons vinegar
1 teaspoon brown sugar
Steamed rice or plain 2 minute noodles, to serve

1. Brown the mince in a searing slow cooker (or frying pan, then transfer to the slow cooker). Stir in the remaining ingredients.
2. Cover and cook on HIGH for 4 hours.
3. Serve with rice or noodles.

Jaime Caillot de Chadbannes

Roast Chicken – Stuffed Full of Flavour

This is a beautifully flavoured whole roast chicken. Serve it with your favourite roast vegetables and gravy, or with a fresh salad in summer. We enjoy this one all year round!

Serves 5 • Preparation 25 mins • Cook 6 hours • Cooker capacity 6 litres

- 1 whole chicken
- 1 brown onion, quartered
- 7 garlic cloves, peeled
- 1 bunch thyme
- 1 lemon, quartered
- 2 tablespoons butter, melted
- 2 teaspoons cracked black pepper

1. Fill the chicken cavity with the onion quarters, whole garlic cloves, thyme sprigs and two of the lemon quarters. Place into the slow cooker, breast side down.
2. Using a small sharp knife make incisions over the surface of the chicken. Mix the melted butter with the black pepper and the juice of 1 lemon quarter. Brush all over the exposed chicken surface and into the holes you've pierced. Save the remaining lemon quarter to garnish the finished dish.
3. Cover and cook on LOW for 6 hours.

NOTE: I slow cook my chicken slightly elevated from the cooking liquids on a trivet, but don't worry if you don't have one.

Paulene Christie

Saucy Pork Cutlets

I wanted to make something quick and easy with pork cutlets in a sauce, so threw this recipe together and it was an amazing success.

Serves 2 • Preparation 5 mins • Cook 3½ hours • Cooker capacity 3.5 litres

Spray oil
280 g (10 oz) apple sauce
2 tablespoons brown sugar
2 pork cutlets

1. Spray the slow cooker bowl with oil. Mix the apple sauce and brown sugar and place into the slow cooker. Add the cutlets and turn to coat in the sauce.
2. Cover and cook on LOW for 3½ hours.

NOTE: This recipe is easily adjustable and can be doubled but the time should stay the same. I served with potato bake and a salad.

Stacey Nanson

BBQ Sausages

BBQ sausages are a favourite. Serve on a bed of pasta and enjoy!

Serves 3–4 • Preparation 5–10 mins • Cook 7–8 hours • Cooker capacity 3.5 litres

1 onion, finely chopped
125 g (4½ oz) butter
1 cup tomato sauce (ketchup)
½ cup vinegar
¼ cup brown sugar
1 tablespoon Worcestershire sauce
1 teaspoon mustard powder
1 teaspoon salt
1 teaspoon paprika
12 sausages
Pasta, to serve

1. Combine all the ingredients except the sausages in the slow cooker. Stir until well combined. Add sausages to sauce.
2. Cover and cook on LOW for 7–8 hours. Serve on a bed of pasta.

Rhianna Pittaway

Chicken Fried Rice

I thought I'd have a go one day and make my very own chicken fried rice. My crew absolutely loved it and I have been making this dish ever since.

Serves 4–6 • Preparation 30 mins • Cook 4–6 hours • Cooker capacity 6 litres

- 2 cups rice
- 1 tablespoon sesame oil
- ½ BBQ chicken, meat shredded
- 1 carrot, grated
- 1 cup sliced spring onions (scallions)
- ½ cup sliced celery
- ½ cup sliced red, yellow and green capsicum (peppers)
- ½ cup frozen peas and corn
- 1 tablespoon each soy, oyster, fish and hoi-sin sauce
- 3 teaspoons chicken stock powder
- 2 eggs
- ½ cup milk
- 2 heaped teaspoons butter

1. Cook the rice as directed until tender. Drain well. Place oil, rice, chicken, carrot, spring onions, celery, capsicum and peas and corn into the slow cooker, then stir in the sauces.
2. Cover, putting a tea towel (dish towel) under the lid, and cook on LOW for 4–6 hours (depending on your cooker).
3. Close to serving time, whisk the eggs and milk together. Melt the butter in a frying pan and add the egg mixture. Cook until set, turning once. Transfer to a board and cut into slices.
4. Stir chicken stock powder and omelette into rice mixture, and serve.

NOTE: If you don't want to make omelette make scrambled eggs instead.

Judith Clark

Sausage Bolognese

My children LOVE sausages, so I often look for ways to include them in recipes to keep the little ones happy. I love bolognese, so this was a great way to combine some favourites for all of us. The cut-up sausages end up being like bitesize meatballs, perfect to serve with spaghetti and topped with grated cheese.

Serves 6–8 • Preparation 15 mins • Cook 10 hours • Cooker capacity 3.5 litres

16 pork sausages (Cumberland work well), chopped into bite-sized pieces
500 ml (17 fl oz) jar passata (puréed tomato)
1 cup red wine
1 onion, diced
1 red capsicum (pepper), diced
3 heaped teaspoons basil pesto
3 garlic cloves
1 teaspoon dried oregano
Generous dash of Worcestershire sauce

1. Combine all the ingredients in the slow cooker bowl and mix well.
2. Cover and cook on LOW for 10 hours or longer (it will cook all day or as long as you need).

Joanne Pinnock

Best Baked Beans in the Universe

You'll never eat canned baked beans again after trying this rich and saucy home-made version. Serve it on toast for a nutritious and budget-friendly meal. This recipe is easily adaptable for vegetarians.

Serves 8–10 • Preparation 10 mins + overnight soaking • Cook 8½ hours
Cooker capacity 3–5 litres

- 2 cups navy (haricot) beans
- 1 bacon or ham hock
- 880 g (1 lb 15 oz) can diced tomato
- 2 tablespoons dried oregano
- 2 teaspoons sweet paprika
- 1–2 tablespoons tomato paste (concentrated purée)
- 1 tablespoon ground cumin
- Toast, to serve

1. Soak the beans overnight in 2 litres cold water. Next day, drain the beans and cook in fresh boiling water for 30 minutes. Drain the beans and discard this water.
2. Spread the beans over the bottom of the cooker. Place the bacon or hock on top of the beans and pour the remaining ingredients over.
3. Cook on LOW for 8 hours, stirring occasionally.
4. Lift hock from slow cooker. Discard skin and chop the meat. Stir meat back into bean mixture.
5. Serve on toast for a yummy meal or after school snack. Leftovers can be frozen… if you have any.

NOTE: The meat can be left out if you are vegetarian. The beans MUST be boiled before being added to the slow cooker for food safety.

Jenny Semmler

Pork & Gravy

A simple and easy pork meal, which can be served as a roast with vegetables and gravy, or shredded and served on rolls with salad. It's a perfect 'serve yourself' meal on sports nights, or for a casual get together.

Serves 4–6 • Preparation 5 mins • Cook 8–12 hours • Cooker capacity 5.5 litres

2 kg (4 lb 6 oz) piece pork (any cut, can be slightly smaller or larger)
½ cup gravy powder

1. Place the pork into the slow cooker. Mix the gravy powder with 600 ml (20½ fl oz) water and pour into the slow cooker.
2. Cover and cook on LOW for 8–12 hours.

NOTE: If you want crackling you can remove the pork from the slow cooker and put it in a hot oven until the skin is crisp. I usually just put a piece of pork rind (cheat and buy a pack from the supermarket) in the oven for crackling. Some of our family prefer no crackling, and this covers both options.

You can cook the pork to the lower end of the time frame and serve sliced, or cook for the full time to make pulled pork, with the gravy mixed through.

Felicity Barnett

Tasty Turkey Drumsticks

I had never done turkey in the slow cooker before and was after something that made a nice gravy to go with mashed potato on a cold winter night. I experimented with what I had in the cupboards and came up with this recipe. My two boys, aged 7 and 4, loved it! Make sure to cut the meat off the bone for the little ones.

Serves 4 • Preparation 10 mins • Cook 5–6 hours • Cooker capacity 6 litres

2 turkey drumsticks
2 x 420 g (15 oz) cans condensed cream of chicken soup
1 onion, diced
⅓ cup gravy powder
¼ cup tomato sauce (ketchup)
1 tablespoon Worcestershire sauce
Half 40 g (1½ oz) packet French onion soup mix
1 teaspoon chicken stock powder
1 teaspoon minced garlic

1. Place the turkey drumsticks into the slow cooker. Mix the remaining ingredients together and pour over the drumsticks.
2. Cover and cook on HIGH for 5–6 hours. Give a stir occasionally and roll the drumsticks over.

NOTE: You could transfer these to a baking dish and place into a moderate oven for the last 30 minutes to crisp up.

Tennille Deckert

Corned Silverside

This was my Nana's recipe. I love it on cold nights because it reminds me of when I was a kid!

Serves 4–6 • Preparation 10 mins • Cook 6–8 hours • Cooker capacity 3 litres

1.5 kg (3 lb 5 oz) piece silverside
2 tablespoons vinegar
2 tablespoons golden syrup

1. Put the silverside into the slow cooker and add the vinegar and golden syrup. Pour in 4 cups of water.
2. Cover and cook on LOW for 6–8 hours.

Niki Vercoe-Linn

Creamy Chicken with Herb Gravy

This is a super simple slow cooked chicken in a lush creamy herb gravy. I used fillets but you could use any chicken pieces.

Serves 5 • Preparation 5 mins • Cook 4½ hours • Cooker capacity 6 litres

1 kg (2 lb 3 oz) chicken thigh fillets
1 teaspoon dried rosemary
1 teaspoon dried thyme
24 g (¾ oz) sachet instant supreme or roast chicken gravy
200 ml (7 fl oz) cooking cream
Mashed potato and steamed seasonal veggies, to serve

1. Place the chicken into the slow cooker (whole, or chopped if you prefer). Sprinkle the herbs over the chicken, then sprinkle with the gravy mix. Pour in ½ cup warm water.
2. Cover and cook on LOW for 4 hours.
3. Gently move the chicken around in the dish to disperse any gravy mix still on top, then transfer the chicken to a plate. Add the cream to the slow cooker and whisk to combine well.
4. Return the chicken to the slow cooker. Cover and cook for a further 30 minutes to heat the gravy through.

NOTE: If you like you could also add 2 teaspoons of cornflour in with the cream to thicken the gravy further, but we didn't feel the need to. The cooking cream is important as it resists splitting like normal cream.

Paulene Christie

Slow Cooker Turkey

This is a great way to free up the oven for other things when cooking a big festive meal. The foil helps keep in the heat and moisture for the turkey, so be sure to use it.

Serves 24 • Preparation 5 mins • Cook 8 hours • Cooker capacity 7 litre

Spray oil
5.5 kg (12 lb) turkey
Seasoned salt

1. Lightly spray inside the slow cooker with oil. Season the turkey with seasoned salt and place into the slow cooker. Cover turkey with foil.
2. Cover and cook on LOW for 8 hours.

NOTE: If your turkey was frozen, make sure it has completely thawed before cooking.

Patricia Schulz

Roast Leg of Lamb with Sweet Chilli Sauce

This is the only way my family love their roast lamb. It cooks so tender and juicy.

Serves 4–6 • Preparation 5–10 mins • Cook 8–10 hours • Cooker capacity 6 litres

2 tablespoons olive oil
1.5–2 kg (3 lb 5 oz–4 lb 6 oz) lamb leg
Half 40 g (1½ oz) packet French onion soup mix
4–6 tablespoons sweet chilli sauce

1. Drizzle olive oil into the slow cooker then add the lamb. Sprinkle French onion soup over the lamb then drizzle sweet chilli sauce over the top.
2. Cover, putting a tea towel (dish towel) under the lid, and cook on LOW for 8–10 hours. Turn leg over halfway through cooking time, and baste with the cooking juices occasionally.

NOTE: The pan juices make absolutely wonderful gravy to complement your roast meat.

Judith Clark

Sweet Soy Asian Chicken

These delicious chicken pieces have a sweet Asian flavour! If you love Chinese food like I do, you'll love this one. You could adapt this recipe to use other cuts or fillets of chicken.

Serves 5 • Preparation 10 mins • Cook 4½ hours • Cooker capacity 6 litres

8 chicken thigh cutlets (bone in, skin on)
½ cup kecap manis (Indonesian sweet soy sauce)
2 tablespoons sweet chilli sauce
1 tablespoon minced garlic
1 tablespoon minced ginger
Brown rice and Asian greens, to serve

1. Place the chicken in the slow cooker. Combine the other ingredients and pour over the chicken.
2. Cover and cook on LOW for 4½ hours. If you are around, baste the chicken with sauce occasionally during the cooking time, for a rich final colour.
3. Serve with brown rice and Asian greens.

Paulene Christie

HOME TAKEAWAY

HOME TAKEAWAY

Orange BBQ Chicken

This is a great quick and easy recipe that kids will love!

Serves 4 • Preparation 5 mins • Cook 4 hours • Cooker capacity 6 litres

- 4 chicken breast fillets
- ¾ cup orange marmalade
- ¾ cup BBQ sauce
- 2 tablespoons soy sauce
- 1–2 spring onions, chopped

1. Put the chicken fillets into the slow cooker.
2. Cover and cook on HIGH for 3 hours.
3. Drain the excess liquid from the slow cooker and add the remaining ingredients. Cook for a further 1 hour.

NOTE: This is lovely served with rice.

Corrina Conlan

Hot Dogs Put Together

This is awesome for growing children, full of nutritious vegetables. It's easy to take the mushrooms out after cooking, if the children don't like them. A great meal for family and visitors alike, and even to freeze for another meal.

Serves 4 • Preparation 15 mins • Cook 4 hours • Cooker capacity 5 litre

- 6 hot dogs, cut into bite-sized pieces
- 2 cups chopped mixed vegetables
- 1 sweet potato, chopped
- 500 g (1 lb 2 oz) mushrooms, thickly sliced
- 400 g (14 oz) can diced tomatoes
- 400 g (14 oz) jar tomato pasta sauce
- 1 red onion, chopped

1. Combine all the ingredients in the slow cooker.
2. Cover and cook on HIGH for 4 hours.

NOTE: Replace the hot dogs with sausages if you like.

Sandra Clasby

Sweet Chilli Cashew Chicken

This was a quick 'throw everything we could find left in the fridge' meal. It's a great mix of sweet and spicy that's a winner with both the adults and the toddlers in our house. It's a weekly staple here – the best part being that you can just use whatever vegetables you have on hand.

Serves 4–6 • Preparation 10 mins • Cook 4 hours • Cooker capacity 3.5 litres

500 g (1 lb 2 oz) chicken breast or thigh fillets, chopped
1 red capsicum (pepper), chopped
1 brown onion, chopped
2 carrots, finely chopped
420 g (15 oz) can pineapple pieces in juice
½ cup sweet chilli sauce
Handful of cashews, crushed
2½ cups penne pasta

1. Place the chicken and vegetables into the slow cooker. Add the sweet chilli sauce and pineapple, including the juice. Stir to combine.
2. Cover and cook on LOW for 4 hours.
3. Add cashews about 10 minutes before end of cooking time. Cook pasta on stovetop, then drain and add to slow cooker. Stir to combine, and serve.

NOTE: If there's a bit too much liquid, turn the slow cooker to HIGH for the last ½–1 hour and uncover so the liquid reduces.

Kristen Strange

Slow Cooked Pizza

It seems very unlikely to cook a pizza in a slow cooker but it's totally possible. It's delicious, awesome for the kids and fun if they help out with the toppings. It's great for dinner, school lunches and party snacks. When you cook a pizza in a slow cooker, the possibilities are endless.

Serves 2 • Preparation 10 mins (plus resting) • Cook 1½–2 hours • Cooker capacity 5.5 litres

> 250 g (9 oz) store-bought raw pizza dough (or make your own if you like)
> Plain (all-purpose) flour, for rolling
> Spray oil
> 2 tablespoons pizza sauce
> 1 cup shredded pizza cheese (combined mozzarella/cheddar/parmesan)
> Toppings of your choice, chopped or sliced

1. Take the dough from the packaging and put it in an oiled bowl. Cover with cling wrap or a damp cloth and let it rest for an hour.
2. Roll the dough out on a lightly floured surface to fit the base of the slow cooker. Spray the slow cooker with oil and lay the dough on the base, forming a slightly raised edge.
3. Spread the sauce over the dough, then sprinkle with the cheese and add the toppings.
4. Cover, putting a tea towel (dish towel) under the lid, and cook on HIGH for 1½–2 hours (it depends on how many toppings you added).
5. Use a spatula to help lift out the pizza out and cut into pieces to serve.

NOTE: The big trick is not to go crazy on the toppings, otherwise the pizza will be doughy and cold in the middle, so less is more.

Keith Hechinger

Slow Cooked Shredded Asian Vegetables

Serve this as a side dish at your next BBQ or dinner. It's delicious and easy and because all the vegetables are tender and flavoured the kids eat them happily without fuss. It's a lovely vibrant rainbow of vegetables on your plate! The vegetable amounts could be halved to serve 4 if desired.

Serves 8 as a side dish • Preparation 10 mins • Cook 30 mins • Cooker capacity 6 litres

800 g (1 lb 12 oz) shredded stir-fry vegetables (or shred your own – see note)
1 cup salt-reduced vegetable stock
1–2 tablespoons soy sauce
1 heaped teaspoon minced garlic
1 heaped teaspoon minced ginger

1. Combine all the ingredients in the slow cooker.
2. Cover and cook for 10 minutes on HIGH. Uncover and give the mixture a good stir. Cover, turn down to LOW and cook for a further 20 minutes or until the vegetables are cooked to your liking.

NOTE: If you are preparing your own veggies, I suggest a mixture of these: red cabbage, white cabbage, wombok, carrot, broccoli and spring onions (scallions).

The 30 minutes cooking time is for fine shredded vegetable strips. Larger cuts will need additional cooking time.

Paulene Christie

Sweet Peanut Satay Chicken Skewers

A creamy, mild satay sauce covering delicious chicken skewers, on a bed of white rice. Easy and yummy for all ages.

Serves 4 • Preparation 15 mins • Cook 2 hours • Cooker capacity 5 litres

500 g (1 lb 2 oz) chicken fillets, cubed
400 ml (13½ fl oz) can coconut cream
250 g (9 oz) peanut butter
¼ cup sweet chilli sauce
2 tablespoons honey
1 tablespoon soy sauce
2 teaspoons minced garlic
Steamed white rice, to serve

1. Thread chicken pieces onto 8 wooden skewers and lay on the bottom of the slow cooker (if they are too long, trim the skewers to fit).
2. Mix the other ingredients in a bowl and microwave until the peanut butter has melted. Stir well and pour over the chicken.
3. Cook on HIGH for 2 hours, turning halfway through. Served on a bed of white rice.

Jenny Krahe

Sweet Chilli Dim Sims (Dumplings)

Dim sims are a popular adaptation of Asian dumplings or wontons and are normally found in takeaway shops in Australia. They are also quite cheap to buy frozen from the grocery store. I stumbled across this by accident one day when cleaning out my freezer. I thought they'd be nice with sweet chilli sauce as a snack for my son. Where I am from, dim sims are popular with children and this recipe is liked by kids as well as being easy for children to make. The sweet chilli sauce is generally not too spicy but you can substitute a sweet and sour sauce if you like. The quantity can be easily increased to suit.

Makes 8 • Preparation 5 mins • Cook 1½–2 hours • Cooker capacity 1.5 litres

8 dim sims (thawed if frozen)
⅓ cup sweet chilli sauce

1. Place the dim sims into the slow cooker in a single layer. Combine the sweet chilli sauce with ⅔ cup water. Pour over the dim sims.
2. Cover and cook on HIGH for 1½–2 hours, stirring occasionally.

NOTE: You can replace the chilli sauce with a jar of sweet and sour sauce, or other sauce that you prefer. The overall quantity can be doubled or tripled if using a larger slow cooker. Dim sims can be replaced with any style of filled wonton or gyoza, but sizes vary.

Keryn Wolff

Sweet BBQ Pulled Pork Nachos

This is a favourite with my children. The pork is flavoursome and tender and goes great on nachos.

Serves 6–8 • Preparation 5 mins • Cook 7–8 hours • Cooker capacity 5.5 litres

- 1.5–2 kg (3 lb 5 oz–4 lb 6 oz) pork shoulder, net removed if it has one
- ¾ cup brown sugar
- ¼ cup honey
- ¼ cup soy sauce
- ¼ cup balsamic vinegar
- 1½ cups grated tasty cheese
- Large packet corn chips
- Sour cream, to serve

1. Place pork in the slow cooker. Mix the brown sugar, honey, soy sauce and vinegar and pour over the pork.
2. Cover and cook on LOW for 7–8 hours.
3. Take the pork out of the slow cooker. Remove the fat then use 2 forks to pull the pork into shreds. Return the pork to the slow cooker to coat in sauce.
4. Preheat a grill. Spread the corn chips onto an oven tray and top evenly with pork. Sprinkle with cheese and cook under the grill until cheese has melted. Serve with sour cream.

Lynda Eagleson

WINTER WARMERS

Old Favourite Casserole Chops

My Mum's old-fashioned family casserole recipe warms you to the soul. Melt in the mouth lamb chops and flavour packed gravy are just perfect for cold winter nights.

Serves 2–3 • Preparation 15 mins • Cook 3 hours • Cooker capacity 6 litres

- 6 lamb forequarter chops (or blade steak equivalent)
- 2 brown onions, sliced
- 3–4 tomatoes, thickly sliced
- 2 garlic cloves, minced
- 1–2 chillies, finely chopped (optional)
- ⅓ cup tomato sauce (ketchup)
- ⅓ cup Worcestershire sauce
- ¼ cup brown vinegar
- 1 heaped tablespoon brown sugar
- 1 tablespoon beef stock powder
- 1 tablespoon cornflour (cornstarch)

1. Layer the chops, onions, tomatoes, garlic and chillies in the slow cooker. Combine the sauces, vinegar, sugar, stock powder and 1 cup water. Pour over the meat and veggies.
2. Cover and cook on HIGH for 2½ hours.
3. Mix the cornflour with ¼ cup water in a small bowl until smooth. Stir into the sauce and cook for a further 30 minutes, to thicken.

Tracey Laing

Creamy Chicken Cup-a-Laksa

This is a quick, easy kind of recipe with simple ingredients – a huge success with our kids too! You could swap out the drumsticks for any cut or fillet of chicken you prefer. This has a mild laksa flavour, not spicy, so is very suitable for the whole family.

Serves 5 • Preparation 5 mins • Cook 5 hours • Cooker capacity 6 litres

10 chicken drumsticks
300 ml (10½ fl oz) cooking cream
65 g (2 oz) (2 sachets) Asian laksa soup mix (no water added)
Brown rice or cauliflower mash and steamed green vegetables, to serve

1. Place the chicken into the slow cooker. Combine the cream and soup mix and pour over the chicken.
2. Cover and cook on LOW for 5 hours.
3. Serve with brown rice or cauliflower mash and green veggies.

NOTE: Cooking cream is a pouring-type cream that resists splitting when heated. You could shred the chicken, remove the bones and stir just the meat through the sauce if you prefer.

Paulene Christie

Chicken Potato Pie

I confess … I love chicken. EVERYTHING chicken! Our children do too. While I still enjoy cottage pie and shepherd's pie I wanted to make a chicken version of the same sort of thing and so this recipe was born. Serve with steamed greens if you like.

Serves 5 • Preparation 20 mins • Cook 5 hours • Cooker capacity 6 litres

FILLING
700 g (1 lb 9 oz) chicken thigh fillets
500 g (1 lb 2 oz) mixed diced frozen vegetables (or fresh if you prefer)
1 onion, diced
1 heaped tablespoon chicken stock powder
1 tablespoon fresh thyme leaves
1 tablespoon fresh rosemary leaves
1 tablespoon minced garlic
1 tablespoon mustard
1 teaspoon cracked black pepper
½ teaspoon salt
150 ml (5½ fl oz) cooking cream

TOPPING
5 large potatoes, chopped
2 tablespoons butter
Milk, to mash
⅔ cup grated tasty cheese

1. Place all the filling ingredients into the slow cooker, except for the cream.
2. Cover and cook on LOW for 4 hours. Remove the chicken, shred, then return to the cooker. Stir through the cooking cream and continue cooking on LOW while you prepare the potato topping.
3. Cook the potatoes in a saucepan of boiling water until tender. Drain well, then mash with butter and milk to a smooth consistency. Top the filling with mashed potato and smooth the surface. Scatter with grated cheese and then cook for a further 30 minutes on HIGH to melt the cheese.

NOTE: No water is added to the filling as it will make its own liquid. The cooking cream is important as it resists splitting like normal cream.

Paulene Christie

Beef Stew

Come home to the smell of dinner cooking. I make the best winter beef stew in my slow cooker and it's gluten-free.

Serves 8 • Preparation 15 mins • Cook 6½ hours • Cooker capacity 5.5 litres

- 1–2 packs braising steak
- 3 large parsnips, diced
- 1 pack carrots, sliced
- 1 swede, diced
- 200 g mushrooms, sliced
- 3 stock cubes (I use gluten-free)
- 4–5 heaped tablespoons cornflour
- 4 bay leaves
- Dried mixed herbs, to taste
- Salt and pepper, to taste
- Roast jacket potatoes, to serve

1. Brown the meat and vegetables in a frying pan. Transfer to the slow cooker.
2. Dissolve the stock cubes in ½ cup boiling water. Add to slow cooker, then top up with enough water to cover meat and vegetables.
3. Cook on HIGH for 1½ hours.
4. Mix cornflour with 1 cup cold water and add to stew, stirring well. Stir in bay leaves, herbs, salt and pepper. Cook on LOW for 5 hours, stirring occasionally if you're around.
5. Serve with jacket potatoes.

Emma Drabble

Chicken Soup

This recipe is inspired by hubby's Baka's (grandma's) beloved delish chicken soup. My aim is for the flavour of her soup, with the convenience of the slow cooker. I love this recipe as it can be cooked all day while I'm at work and the kids love it! It's also amazing for fighting those nasty colds in winter! Perfect if you have a lot of time at the end of the day and next to no time in the morning!

Makes 6 litres • Preparation 15 mins • Cook 4–12 hours • Cooker capacity 6 litres

2 chicken breast fillets or 6–8 thigh fillets
4 carrots, ends trimmed
4 celery stalks with leaves (and some extra leaves if available)
2 onions, quartered
2 garlic cloves, chopped
4 tablespoons vegetable stock powder, plus extra to taste
140 g (5 oz) thin dried egg noodles

1. Throw the chicken, carrots, celery, onions, garlic and stock powder into the slow cooker. Add enough water to come about 5 cm (2 inches) from the top.
2. Cover and cook on HIGH for 4 hours or on LOW for up to 12 hours.
3. 30 minutes before serving, turn the slow cooker to HIGH if on LOW. Carefully remove the chicken, carrots, celery and onions. Add the noodles to the slow cooker, cover and cook a further 30 minutes, until tender. Season with freshly ground black pepper and more stock powder to taste.
4. Use 2 forks to shred the chicken and add back to the slow cooker. Roughly mash the vegetables and add back to the slow cooker. Alternatively, serve the chicken and vegetables separately from the broth and noodles for people to help themselves (this is how Baka serves her delicious soup).

NOTE: You could use drumsticks, but I don't find bones to work well for a long slow cooker day.

Kathryn Dijak

Cheesy Potato Soup

This hearty soup is cheap and easy to make, and is a hit with the kids.

Serves 6 • Preparation 10 mins • Cook 8 hours • Cooker capacity 6 litres

6 medium potatoes, peeled and finely chopped
1 onion, finely chopped
½ teaspoon pepper
2 chicken stock cubes
250 g (9 oz) block processed cheese, grated
1 cup cream
Crusty bread, to serve

1. Combine the potatoes, onion and pepper in the slow cooker. Dissolve the stock cubes in 8 cups water and stir in.
2. Cover and cook on LOW for 7 hours. Stir in the cheese and cream and cook for 1 hour further.
3. Serve with crusty bread.

NOTE: Make sure you chop your potatoes into small pieces as they can take a long time to cook.

Fiona Masters

Taco Mushroom Sausages

This is a quick and easy dinner, great for cold nights. We serve ours with creamy mashed potato.

Serves 4–5 • Preparation 10 minutes • Cook 4 hours • Cooker capacity 6.5 litres

2 potatoes, quartered
8 sausages
30 g (1 oz) taco seasoning sachet
420 g (15 oz) can condensed cream of mushroom soup
425 g (15 oz) can champignon mushrooms
1 brown onion, thickly sliced
1 teaspoon minced garlic

1. Place the potatoes into the slow cooker. Lightly brown the sausages in a frying pan then place on top of the potatoes.
2. Dissolve the taco seasoning in 1 cup of water and add to the slow cooker along with the remaining ingredients.
3. Cover and cook on HIGH for 4 hours. If you are around, stir once or twice during cooking time.

NOTE: Add other veggies if you like. You can keep the sausages whole or cut them up, it's up to you.

Luke & Melissa Shenton

Slow Cooked Saucy Shanks

I wanted to create a family friendly slow cooked shank recipe with a 'moreish' flavour that would have the whole family coming back for more. Combining all our favourite flavours I came up with this recipe. Even your fussiest eaters will be licking the plate clean.

Serves 4 • Preparation 15 mins • Cook 6 hours • Cooker capacity 6 litres

4 lamb shanks
1 carrot, chopped
1 onion, chopped
2 garlic cloves, minced
1 red chilli, chopped
400 g (14 oz) can diced tomatoes
420 g (15 oz) can condensed tomato soup
1 cup beef stock
40 g (1½ oz) packet French onion soup mix
1 tablespoon Worcestershire sauce
1 tablespoon dried Italian herbs
Mashed potatoes and steamed vegetables, to serve

1. Place the shanks into the slow cooker. Top with the carrot, onion, garlic and chilli.
2. Mix the rest of the ingredients together in a bowl and pour over the shanks.
3. Cover and cook on LOW for 6 hours.
4. Serve on a bed of creamy mash with a side of vegetables.

Shaeden Galpin

Creamy Country Chicken Casserole

Chicken with leek, potato, carrots and a creamy sauce ... a complete meal from your slow cooker with no extra pots, pans or mess! Winner winner chicken dinner! This has roast chicken dinner flavours the kids will love.

Serves 5 • Preparation 10 mins • Cook 5 hours • Cooker capacity 6 litres

3 washed potatoes, cut into small chunks
1 leek, sliced
10 chicken drumsticks
1 bunch baby (Dutch) carrots, trimmed
300 ml (10½ fl oz) cooking cream
24 g (¾ oz) sachet chicken gravy
Crusty bread rolls, to serve

1. Place the potato and leeks over the base of the slow cooker bowl. Lay the chicken drumsticks over them, then arrange the carrots on top.
2. Combine the cream and gravy mix in a jug then pour over. Season with salt and pepper.
3. Cover and cook on HIGH for 5 hours.
4. To serve, carefully transfer the carrots and chicken to serving plates. Use a slotted spoon to lift out the potatoes and add them to the serving plates. Give the sauce a quick whisk then ladle over the chicken and veggies. Serve with bread rolls to mop up the gravy.

NOTE: I kept the potato chunks fairly small to ensure they cooked through. This would also work with boneless chicken, and you could add other vegetables if you wished. The cooking cream is important as it resists splitting like normal cream.

Paulene Christie

Kath's Beef Stew

This stew is delicious and my little grandsons love it. It's the one dish in my household that we all eat – my girls love it served with puff pastry rectangles. I converted this dish to the slow cooker and refuse to go back. It's perfect for a cold winter night, and leftovers are suitable to turn into pies.

Serves 6 • Preparation 15–20 mins • Cook 6–8 hours • Cooker capacity 5 litres

- 1 kg (2 lb 3 oz) diced beef
- 1 onion, diced
- 1 tablespoon olive oil (optional)
- 4 carrots, diced
- 6 potatoes, diced
- 4 celery stalks, diced
- 40 g (1½ oz) packet French onion soup mix
- ¼ cup Worcestershire sauce
- 100 g (3½ oz) tomato paste, or ⅓ cup tomato sauce (ketchup)
- 400 g (14 oz) can diced tomatoes
- 2 cups frozen peas
- 2 tablespoon gravy powder

1. If you like, brown the beef and onion in the oil in a frying pan. Otherwise, place straight into the slow cooker with the vegetables, soup mix, Worcestershire sauce, tomato paste and tomatoes. Fill the empty can with water, swish around and add to slow cooker.
2. Cover and cook on LOW for 6–8 hours. Add the peas 30 minutes before end of cooking time.
3. At the end of cooking time, stir in the gravy powder to thicken the gravy.

NOTE: Add other veggies like turnip or swede if you like.

Kathryn Ryles

Shredded Beef Chilli Con Carne

This is a great alternative to the usual chilli made with minced beef. This is NOT a hot chilli (even my 4 year old enjoyed this one) so if you like it hot consider adding more chilli powder. Serve on rice or corn chips, with a dollop of sour cream on the side.

Serves 6–8 • Preparation 15 mins • Cook 5 hours • Cooker capacity 6 litres

- 1.5 kg (3 lb 5 oz) blade steaks (or other stewing-type cut of beef)
- 1 large onion, diced
- 1 red capsicum (pepper), diced
- 1 red chilli, deseeded and diced
- 400 g (14 oz) can kidney beans, rinsed and drained
- 400 g (14 oz) can diced tomatoes
- 2 tablespoons tomato paste
- 1 tablespoon minced garlic
- 1 teaspoon ground cumin
- 1 teaspoon smoked paprika
- ½ teaspoon dried oregano
- ¼ teaspoon chilli powder

1. Lay the whole steaks in the base of the slow cooker. Add the onion, capsicum and chilli. Combine all the other ingredients and pour over.
2. Cover and cook on HIGH for 4 hours, or until the meat is falling apart tender.
3. Remove the steaks, shred with 2 forks, and return to the slow cooker. Mix to combine well and continue to cook, covered, for a further 1 hour on LOW.

Paulene Christie

Pulled Roast Lamb In Gravy

A beautiful slow cooked roast leg of lamb, pulled then finished in a lush rich meat gravy! This is great for family roast dinners, parties or self-serve food at functions. It's lovely and tender for little ones.

Serves 8–10 • Preparation 15 mins • Cook 8 hours • Cooker capacity 6 litres

2 kg (4 lb 6 oz) lamb leg
1 heaped tablespoon minced garlic
2 tablespoons mint sauce
1–2 tablespoons 'lamb herbs' mix (see note)
50 g (1¾ oz) rich meat gravy powder (or your favourite roast lamb gravy)
Roast veggies or bread rolls, to serve

1. Place the lamb leg into the slow cooker and pierce all over with a sharp knife. Season with salt and pepper. Spread the minced garlic all over the top surface of the lamb and rub in well. Drizzle with the mint sauce and sprinkle with the herbs.
2. Cook on LOW for 7½ hours (no liquid is needed, it will soon make plenty of its own).
3. Remove the bone from the lamb and shred the meat into the juices. Add the gravy powder and 1 cup of water.
4. Cover and cook for a further 30 minutes or until the gravy is lovely and thick. Serve with your favourite roast vegetables or let others self serve onto bread rolls at your next party.

NOTE: Lamb herbs mix is a mixture of dried rosemary, garlic, marjoram, thyme, oregano, mint and basil. Look for it with the herbs and spices at the supermarket.

Paulene Christie

Nanna's Chicken Casserole

This recipe is so close to my heart. My best friend Heather made me this beautiful dish for my birthday. I asked where she got the recipe, or did she make it up. She replied that she grew up with its beautiful aromas wafting through her Nana's house when she was a kid. Her Nan is just an absolute beautiful soul, so caring and humble. She used to make this beautiful simple dish all the time at the children's request, as it was an all time favourite. I just had to share it with my slow cooking family. I know you'll all just love it!!

Serves 4–6 • Preparation 15–20 mins • Cook 4 or 6 hours • Cooker capacity 7 litres

8–10 pieces short cut bacon, diced
1–2 kg (2 lb 3 oz–4 lb 6 oz) chicken breast or thigh fillet, chopped
Minced garlic (fresh or from a jar), to taste
4 x 420 g cans condensed cream of chicken soup
Mashed potato, to serve

1. Brown the bacon in a large frying pan. Transfer to the slow cooker. Brown the chicken in the same pan, adding the garlic for the last minute. Add to the slow cooker.
2. Stir in the soup, but do not add any water.
3. Cover and cook on HIGH for 4 hours or LOW for 6 hours.
4. Serve over mashed potato, seasoned with freshly ground black pepper.

Tyneil Fear

Roast Beef with Rich Gravy

Serves 6 • Preparation 15 mins • Cook 6–8 hours • Cooker capacity 6 litres

2 kg piece beef blade or topside roast
1 large onion, quartered
1½ tablespoons American-style mustard
27 g (1 oz) sachet instant roast meat gravy powder

SPICE RUB
1½ teaspoons smoked paprika
¾ teaspoon garlic powder
½ teaspoon pink Himalayan salt
½ teaspoon cracked black pepper
¼ teaspoon ground cumin

1. Place the beef into the slow cooker and use a small sharp knife to pierce some holes all over the top surface. Arrange the onion around the beef.
2. Spread the mustard over the top of the beef. Combine the rub ingredients and rub onto and into the surface of the beef.
3. Cover and cook on HIGH for 4 hours then LOW for 2 hours (see note).
4. Carefully lift the beef from the cooker and place onto a board or platter. Cover with foil and set aside to rest. Use a slotted spoon to remove the onion, and discard it. Add the gravy powder to the cooking juices in the slow cooker and whisk to combine well. Cover and cook on HIGH for 10–15 minutes, until thickened.

NOTE: You could cook this on AUTO for 7 hours, or LOW for 8 hours.

Paulene Christie

DINNER HITS

DINNER HITS

Swedish-style Meatballs

I love the meatballs you can buy from Ikea, so I thought I would work out my own recipe to recreate the taste. Simple and easy to make, this is really tasty. This recipe makes loads of lush sauce so you could easily add more meatballs. It's great served with hasselback potatoes.

Serves 4 • Preparation 10 mins • Cook 8 hours • Cooker capacity 3.5 litres

420 g (15 oz) can cream of chicken soup
1 cup beef stock
¼ cup Worcestershire sauce
2 tablespoons HP sauce
1 teaspoon garlic salt
1 teaspoon onion salt
Good sprinkle of allspice
24 purchased pork meatballs
2 heaped tablespoons sour cream

1. Mix all the ingredients (except the meatballs and sour cream) together in the slow cooker bowl. Add the meatballs.
2. Cover and cook on LOW for 7½ hours. Stir in the sour cream and cook for a further 30 minutes.

Joanne Pinnock (Simpson)

Milo's Creamy Pesto Chicken Meatballs

These are my favourite meatballs (other than the ones you get at IKEA). They're easy to make and really yummy with spaghetti or fettuccine.

Serves 6 • Preparation 10 mins • Cook 6 hours • Cooker capacity 6 litres

8 chicken sausages
3 tablespoons basil pesto
1 cup cooking cream
1 cup frozen peas
Spaghetti or fettuccine and salad, to serve

1. Cut the sausages in half and squeeze 2 portions out of each half. Roll into balls and place into the slow cooker.
2. Mix the pesto and cream together and pour over the meatballs.
3. Cover and cook on LOW for 6 hours, adding peas 30 minutes before the end of cooking.
4. Serve with spaghetti or fettuccine and a simple side salad.

Fiona Masters

Cheesy Chicken One Pot Pasta

An easy, cheesy, one-pot, budget friendly recipe: cheesy chicken pasta with peas and corn. This is one the whole family will enjoy! And a complete one-pot meal means less mess to clean up after dinner.

Serves 5 • Preparation 10 mins • Cook 5 hours 10 mins • Cooker capacity 6 litres

1 kg (2 lb 3 oz) chicken thigh fillets, diced
420 g (15 oz) can condensed cream of chicken soup
250 g (9 oz) frozen peas and corn mix
200 g (7 oz) small elbow pasta, raw
200 g (7 oz) grated tasty cheese

1. Combine the chicken, soup and vegetables in the slow cooker.
2. Cover and cook on LOW for 4½ hours.
3. Add the pasta, cover and cook for a further 30 minutes. Stir well then add the cheese. Cover and cook for 10 more minutes.

Paulene Christie

Herbed Chicken

A lovely herb-filled, tender chicken recipe designed to surprise my wife who follows a low-carb way of eating – but it ended up being a huge hit with the kids too.

Serves 8 • Preparation 20 mins • Cook 6 hours • Cooker capacity 6 litres

- 2 kg (4 lb 6 oz) chicken drumsticks
- 2 garlic cloves, minced
- 1 cup sliced spring onions (scallions)
- 4 large mushrooms, diced
- ¼ red capsicum (pepper), sliced
- 1 tablespoon salt-reduced soy sauce
- 1 tablespoon Worcestershire sauce
- 1 tablespoon chopped fresh oregano
- 1 tablespoon chopped fresh basil
- 1 tablespoon chopped fresh garlic chives
- 2–3 sprigs fresh thyme

1. Brown the chicken drumsticks briefly with the garlic in a searing slow cooker or on the stovetop.
2. Combine the chicken with all the other ingredients in the slow cooker. Cover and cook on HIGH for 1 hour then LOW for 5 hours. Pull the meat from the bones, or serve whole if you prefer.

Simon Christie

Sticky Steakhouse Ribs

Nothing says 'good ribs' like sticky little faces licking their fingers after devouring! Our kids love these ribs served with chunky chips and slaw for a fun weekend meal.

Serves 4–6 • Preparation 15 mins • Cook 6 or 8 hours • Cooker capacity 6 litres

- 1.5 kg beef spare ribs (the really meaty kind of ribs on wide flat bones)
- 1 onion, finely grated
- ⅔ cup steak sauce (your favourite)
- 2 tablespoons yellow mustard
- 2 tablespoons brown sugar
- 1 tablespoon minced garlic
- 1 teaspoon smoked paprika

1. Place the ribs into the slow cooker. Combine all other the ingredients to make the marinade. Reserve ½ cup of the marinade for later, and pour the remaining marinade over the ribs.
2. Cook on AUTO for 6 hours or LOW for 8 hours.
3. Carefully transfer the super tender cooked ribs to an oven tray and baste with the reserved marinade. Cook under a hot grill for about 10 minutes or until browned and glazed with the sticky sauce. Don't put the meat too close to the heat source, and take care that it doesn't burn!

Paulene Christie

Stroganoff

This is a versatile stroganoff recipe that has become a favourite, enjoyed all year round.

Serves 4–6 • Preparation 15 mins • Cook 7½ hours • Cooker capacity 3.5 litres

1 kg (2 lb 3 oz) beef, chicken or pork, cut into strips
850 g (1¾ oz) mixed mushrooms (button, Swiss brown, oyster), quartered
1 onion, finely sliced
3 garlic cloves, minced
1 cup sour cream
½ cup vegetable stock
2 tablespoons cornflour (cornstarch)
2 tablespoons tomato sauce (ketchup)
2 teaspoons Worcestershire sauce
1½ teaspoons paprika
¼ teaspoon cracked black pepper
250 g (9 oz) cream cheese, chopped, at room temperature
3 cups baby spinach leaves
Rice noodles, pasta, steamed rice or mashed potato, to serve

1. Place the meat, mushrooms, onion and garlic into the slow cooker.
2. Combine the sour cream, stock, cornflour, sauces and spices in a jug. Pour the mixture into the slow cooker.
3. Cover and cook on LOW for 7 hours.
4. Stir the cream cheese and spinach through, cover and cook for a further 30 minutes or until the cheese has melted through and the spinach has wilted. Serve with rice noodles, pasta, rice or mashed potato.

NOTE: If using pork, I like to serve with crackling on top. Buy pork rind from your butcher or supermarket and place on a tray in a hot oven to crackle.

Felicity Barnett

Tortellini in Tomato Basil Sauce

I wanted to make tortellini for dinner but only had some that was frozen and all of the recipes that I could find said to use fresh. So I thought I'd throw the frozen pasta in at the beginning and see what happened. The pasta holds together well and is a quick, easy and delicious meal the whole family loves.

Serves 4 • Preparation 5 mins • Cook 3–4 hours • Cooker capacity 6.5 litres

625 g (1 lb 6 oz) packet frozen tortellini
420 g (15 oz) can tomato soup
1 onion, chopped
Large handful of diced bacon
2 teaspoons minced garlic
1 teaspoon dried basil
1 teaspoon dried parsley
½ cup thickened cream

1. Place all the ingredients except the cream into the slow cooker and stir to combine.
2. Cover and cook on LOW for 3–4 hours. 15 minutes before serving, stir in the cream.

NOTE: If you want to use fresh (chilled) tortellini instead of frozen, add to the slow cooker 30 minutes before serving.

Angela Dalgleish

Texas BBQ Shredded Chicken

This pulled chicken recipe is versatile, family friendly and budget friendly too! Serve it on baked potatoes, on pizza, on pasta, in salads, on burgers ... on anything you like! Nice and easy for the kids to cook too.

Serves 4 • Preparation 10 mins • Cook 4 hours • Cooker capacity 6 litres

700 g (1 lb 9 oz) skinless chicken thigh fillets
1 red onion, finely diced
40 g (1½ oz) BBQ spice rub (see note)
1 tablespoon minced garlic
1 cup chicken stock

1. Place the chicken fillets into the slow cooker. Add the onion, spice rub and garlic and mix well to coat the chicken. Pour over the chicken stock
2. Cover and cook on LOW for 4 hours.
3. Shred the chicken and stir into the sauce.

NOTE: Look in the spice aisle at the supermarket for BBQ spice rub mixtures.

Paulene Christie

Sticky Vegetarian Sausages

I used the classic 'sausage and beans' as inspiration for this great way to get my little carnivores to eat less meat. The veggie sausages have a sticky texture when cooked hence the name, and my kids love it because of that. This can be a complete stand alone meal, served with rice or bread.

Serves 4 • Preparation 20 mins • Cook 3 hours • Cooker capacity 5 litres

6 vegetarian sausages
1 onion, chopped
1 garlic clove, minced
2 cups tomato passata (puréed tomato), or to taste
400 g (14 oz) can tomatoes
220 g (7½ oz) can baked beans
1 teaspoon curry paste, or to taste (optional)
2 blocks (60 g/2 oz) frozen spinach

1. Brown the sausages in a frying pan then place into the slow cooker (I find this necessary so they don't fall apart). Brown the onion and garlic and add to the slow cooker.
2. Combine the passata, tomatoes, baked beans and curry paste to your desired consistency and taste. Pour into the slow cooker.
3. Cover and cook on HIGH for 2½ hours. Add spinach and cook for a further 30 minutes.

NOTE: I find the baked beans and curry paste provide enough salt and seasoning for my kids and choose not to add anything extra.

Antonia O'Dowd-Booth

Hearty Beef & Pasta Stew

This was originally a 'throw-together' dinner made with what I had on hand. The kids liked it so much that I have made it several times since.

Serves 6 • Preparation 10 mins • Cook 6 hours • Cooker capacity 7 litres

700 g (1 lb 9 oz) gravy or chuck beef, cubed
8 slices short cut bacon, chopped
4 medium potatoes, chopped
2 carrots, thickly sliced
1½ teaspoons onion powder (or 1 large onion, chopped)
¼ cup minced garlic
¼ cup gravy powder
2 teaspoons beef stock powder
2 x 400 g (14 oz) cans diced tomatoes
2 tablespoons Worcestershire sauce
250 g (9 oz) small soup pasta (such as risoni)
1 bunch broccolini, chopped

1. If you like, brown the beef and bacon in a little oil in a frying pan first. Combine beef and bacon in the slow cooker with the remaining ingredients, except for the pasta and broccolini. Season with freshly ground black pepper and stir well.

2. Cover and cook on HIGH for 2 hours then LOW for 3½ hours (or cook for 7½ hours on LOW). Add the pasta and broccolini and cook for a further 30 minutes, until pasta is tender.

NOTE: Any vegetable you have on hand can be added. Instead of the canned tomatoes, you could use a 700 g (1 lb 9 oz) jar of passata. Wash out the jar with about ½ cup of water and add that as well. Once the pasta has been added, if the stew becomes too dry just add a little hot water and mix well. This is a thick stew and can be eaten on its own or with crusty bread rolls.

Karen Stuckings

Loaded Spanish Bake

Think of this as a Spanish potato bake with one of my favourite combinations – chicken and chorizo! Based on vegetables, topped with meat then eggs, it's a one pot meal everyone can enjoy. If you have little children who might find chorizo too spicy you can leave it out.

Serves 5 • Preparation 10 mins • Cook 5 hours 15 mins • Cooker capacity 6 litres

Spray oil
5 medium washed potatoes, thinly sliced
400 g (14 oz) can diced tomatoes
2 teaspoons minced garlic
1 teaspoon dried oregano
2 teaspoons chicken stock powder
1 red onion, sliced
400 g (14 oz) chicken breast fillet
125 g (4½ oz) chorizo sausage, sliced
3 eggs

1. Spray the slow cooker bowl with oil. Layer the potato slices on the bottom of the slow cooker bowl. Combine the tomatoes, garlic and oregano and pour over the potato. Sprinkle with chicken stock powder, then spread the onion slices over.
2. Cut the chicken breast in half lengthways, then slice each half into thin strips. Spread the chicken slices over the onions, then arrange the chorizo slices over the chicken.
3. Cover and cook on HIGH for 5 hours.
4. Make 3 indentations along the top of the ingredients and crack an egg into each one. Cover and cook for about another 15 minutes, until the eggs set.

Paulene Christie

Tomato Sauce & Brown Sugar Chicken

This is a dish that was passed down by my Mum. It was a favourite when we were kids! You can use a whole chicken, chicken wings, any type of chicken! It tastes great and it's fun for kids.

Serves a family • Preparation 15 mins • Cook 4–8 hours • Cooker capacity 6 litres

Whole chicken, or wings or drumsticks
1 cup tomato sauce (ketchup)
1 cup brown sugar
Soy sauce, to taste
Minced garlic, to taste

1. Combine the tomato sauce, sugar and soy sauce and garlic to your taste.
2. Rub the marinade into the chicken, then place it into the slow cooker. Pour leftover marinade over the chicken.
3. Cover and cook on HIGH for 3–4 hours.
4. Make sure the chicken is fully cooked (juices will run clear). Lift out and serve. If you like, transfer to an oven dish and bake at 180°C (350°F) for a few minutes to make the skin crisp.

NOTE: Make a sling out of foil to make it easier to get the chicken out once cooked. You could cook it on LOW for 6–8 hours if you prefer.

Lucy Halzhauser

Cheesy One Pot Sausage & Veggie Pasta

A complete child friendly meal served right from your slow cooker. This is sausages, pasta and vegetables with a cheesy twist! Kids of all ages will love this one – even toddlers can get their self-feeding perfected with this easy meal.

Serves 6 • Preparation 15 mins • Cook 5 hours 10 mins • Cooker capacity 6 litres

500 g (1 lb 2 oz) diced mixed vegetables (I used a bag of frozen veggies)
16 pork chipolata sausages, halved (or 8 regular pork sausages cut into quarters)
100 g (3½ oz) diced bacon
400 g (14 oz) can diced tomatoes
½ cup BBQ sauce
1 cup macaroni pasta
1 cup grated tasty cheese
Parmesan cheese, optional, to serve

1. Place the vegetables into the slow cooker. Add the sausages and bacon. Combine the tomatoes, BBQ sauce and ½ cup of water and pour over.
2. Cover and cook on LOW for 4½ hours.
3. Add 1 cup hot water and the pasta. Cover and cook on LOW for a further 40 minutes or until pasta is cooked to your liking. Keep an eye on it during this stage, as if your cooker is hotter than others it may need extra water. Just add ½ cup at a time if you think it's needed.
4. Stir the tasty cheese through then serve. You can also top with a sprinkle of grated Parmesan cheese if you like.

Paulene Christie

Honey Mustard Sausage Pot

This is an old family favourite that has been converted from oven to slow cooker. My boys made this recipe up years ago so full credit goes to them.

Serves 5 • Preparation 15 mins • Cook 8¼ hours • Cooker capacity 5.5 litres

1 kg (2 lb 3 oz) sausages, diced (any kind)
1 onion, sliced
2 tablespoons cornflour (cornstarch)
2 tablespoons grainy mustard
2 tablespoons tomato paste (concentrated purée)
1 tablespoon soy sauce
5 teaspoons honey
2 tablespoons cornflour (cornstarch), extra
Mashed potato or sweet potato for topping
Milk, for brushing

1. Combine sausages and onion in the slow cooker. Mix the cornflour and 1 cup water in a large jug until smooth, then add the remaining ingredients and stir to combine. Pour over the sausages.
2. Cover and cook on LOW for 8 hours. About 30 minutes before the end of cooking time, mix the extra cornflour with ⅓ cup water and stir into the sauce to thicken (it will be very thick).
3. Preheat the oven to 200°C (400°F). Transfer mixture to a pie dish. Top with mash and brush with milk. Place into the oven and cook just long enough to brown the top.

NOTE: Add some frozen vegetables towards the end of cooking time, if you like. If you choose not to brown the sausages first (I don't) I find using a serrated knife to dice the sausages works really well.

Katherine Barron

Cantonese Pork Pieces

A tasty pork recipe that's beautiful and tender after slow cooking. Use any cut of pork you prefer but make sure it's one with some fat and not super-lean, so the end result is moist and delicious. This flavour is mild enough for the whole family – not spicy.

Serves 5 • Preparation 15 mins • Cook 5½ hours • Cooker capacity 6 litres

1.5 kg (3 lb 5 oz) pork scotch fillet steaks, cubed
1 large red onion, sliced
⅓ cup hoi sin sauce
2 tablespoons salt-reduced soy sauce
1 tablespoon sesame oil
1 teaspoon minced ginger
1 teaspoon minced garlic
1 tablespoon cornflour (optional)

1. Place the pork and onion into the slow cooker. Combine the remaining ingredients (except the cornflour) and pour over. Stir to combine
2. Cover and cook on LOW for 5 hours.
3. If you want to thicken the sauce, mix the cornflour with 1 tablespoon of water. Stir into the pork mixture, then cover and cook for a further 30 minutes.

Paulene Christie

Creamy Mexican Chicken

A slow cooked creamy Mexican shredded chicken dish the whole family can enjoy! If your children prefer chicken fillets to bone-in pieces you can use those instead. This recipe is amazing served with fresh steamed green vegetables, rice, or even pasta!

Serves 5 • Preparation 15 mins • Cook 4½ hours • Cooker capacity 6 litres

5 chicken maryland pieces (about 1.5 kg (3 lb 5 oz)
250 g (9 oz) block cream cheese, cubed
35 g (1 oz) packet taco seasoning mix
1 tablespoon cornflour (cornstarch)
150 ml (5½ fl oz) cooking cream

1. Place the chicken into the slow cooker. Toss the cream cheese over the chicken and sprinkle the taco seasoning mix over the top.
2. Cover and cook on LOW for 4 hours.
3. Carefully lift out the chicken pieces, pull the meat from the bones and set aside (discard bones).
4. Give the sauce a REALLY good whisk while the chicken is out, to break down any remaining cream cheese lumps. Mix the cornflour into the cream until smooth, then whisk into the sauce. Return the chicken to the cooker, cover and cook for a further 30 minutes.

NOTE: The cooking cream is important as it resists splitting like normal cream.

Paulene Christie

Chicken with Asparagus & Bacon

A fast and easy chicken dinner the whole family will love! It's also inexpensive enough to feed your family of 4 for under $10. If you don't think your children will like asparagus you can vary the flavour of the creamed soup. Try chicken or mushroom.

Serves 4 • Preparation 5 mins • Cook 5 hours • Cooker capacity 6 litres

8 chicken drumsticks
400 g (14 oz) can condensed cream of asparagus soup (no water added)
1 onion, diced
100 g (3½ oz) diced bacon
1 tablespoon minced garlic
Steamed rice, to serve

1. Place the chicken into the slow cooker. Combine all the other ingredients and pour over the chicken.
2. Cook on LOW for 5 hours.
3. Serve with steamed rice.

NOTE: After 4 hours I took the chicken meat off the bones and returned the meat to the slow cooker, but you can leave drumsticks whole if you prefer.

Paulene Christie

Sweet Potato & Corn Soup

I wanted to try a sweet potato soup but my daughter wasn't keen. After discussing what she felt like, she came up with this. Wanting it to be a smooth rather than clear soup, she decided to blend the vegetables towards the end. The result was a lovely sweet winter soup.

Serves 6–8 • Preparation 10 mins • Cook 8½–9½ hours • Cooker capacity 3.5 litres

650 g sweet potato, diced
3 cups corn kernels
2 bay leaves
¼ teaspoon dried thyme
4½ cups vegetable stock
Pinch cracked pepper
Pinch salt

1. Place the stock, sweet potato, 2 cups corn kernels, bay leaves, thyme and pepper into the slow cooker.
2. Cover and cook for 8–9 hours on LOW.
3. Transfer the sweet potato and corn to a food processor with 1 cup of the liquid and blend until smooth. Return to the slow cooker and stir through the remaining 1 cup corn kernels. Add salt if required and continue cooking until corn is heated through.

NOTE: Those who can have dairy may like to serve with a dollop of sour cream.

Felicity Barnett and Susannah Durbidge

Creamy Chicken & Chorizo Pasta

I wanted something that would be tasty and easy to prepare while hubby was at cricket, using only ingredients that I happened to have in the pantry, so that I could effectively take the day off. I was watching my friend's young child for the day and she was sleeping so it had to be quick too.

Serves 4–6 • Preparation 10 mins • Cook 4 hours • Cooker capacity 6.5 litres

500 g (1 lb 2 oz) chicken breast or thigh fillet, diced
1 or 2 chorizo sausages, thinly sliced
420 g (15 oz) can condensed cream of chicken soup
Handful of diced bacon
1 onion, finely diced (so kids can't find it)
2 teaspoons minced garlic
2 teaspoons chicken stock powder (optional)
Few large handfuls pasta

1. Combine all the ingredients except the pasta in the slow cooker and stir well.
2. Cover and cook on LOW for 3 hours. Stir in the pasta, add ¾ cup of water and cook for a further 1 hour, or until pasta is tender, adding more water if needed.

NOTE: If you have more people to feed just use more chicken and more pasta, and increase liquids accordingly.

Angela Dalgleish

Satay Chicken & Spinach

This beautiful saucy satay is great over pasta or with vegetables. I wanted a low-carb meal that I could share with my whole family and this hit the spot perfectly. If your kids aren't fans of spinach you could leave it out, or swap it for some cooked broccoli or other green veggies stirred through at the end.

Serves 5 • Preparation 10 mins • Cook 4 hours • Cooker capacity 6 litres

- 1 kg (2 lb 3 oz) chicken thigh fillets, diced
- 1 cup smooth peanut butter
- 1 teaspoon curry powder
- 2 tablespoons sugar-free sweet chilli sauce
- 300 ml (10½ fl oz) cooking cream
- 120 g (4½ oz) baby spinach leaves

1. Place the chicken into the slow cooker. Whisk the peanut butter and 1 cup hot water in a large jug. Add the curry powder, sweet chilli sauce and cream to the jug and stir to combine. Pour over the chicken.
2. Cover and cook on LOW for 4 hours. About 10 minutes before the chicken is ready, add the spinach. Cover and cook a further 10 minutes, until wilted.

NOTE: This is beautiful served with a side of mashed potato and steamed veggies.

Paulene Christie

Curried Sausages

Here is a super simple, mild curry for the whole family to enjoy. For those who like a bit of extra spice, add chilli flakes to individual bowls once served. Delicious!

Serves 6–8 • Preparation time 15 mins • Cook 4–5 hours • Cooker capacity 6 litres

16 sausages
4 cups chicken stock
400 g (14 oz) can diced tomatoes
3 carrots, chopped
1 onion, chopped
2 tablespoons curry powder
1 teaspoon minced garlic
1–2 cups frozen peas, beans & corn
400 ml (13½ fl oz) can coconut cream
Steamed rice and naan bread, to serve

1. Blanch the sausages in a saucepan of boiling water for 5 minutes. Chop and place into the slow cooker. Add all other ingredients except for the frozen vegetables and the coconut cream.
2. Cover and cook on LOW for 4–5 hours. Add the frozen vegetables and coconut cream in the last hour of cooking time.
3. Serve on rice with naan bread on the side.

NOTE: You can thicken this with a little cornflour mixed with water if you like. I often add potatoes and sweet potato. You can add any veggies of choice to this delicious, versatile curry.

Garry Richter

Fast 'n' Simple Marinated Wings – 3 Ways

You have your choice of marinades here – and whichever one you choose, it will be an easy 4 ingredient recipe. It is great finger food for a party, or a simple meal served with rice and salad or vegetables.

Serves 4 • Preparation 5 mins + marinating time • Cook 4 hours • Cooker capacity 1.5 litres

1 kg (2 lb 3 oz) chicken wings

MARINADE 1
¼ cup coconut aminos sauce or soy sauce
¼ cup honey
1 tablespoon apple cider vinegar

MARINADE 2
¼ cup coconut aminos sauce or soy sauce
¼ cup honey
1 small chilli, finely diced

MARINADE 3
1½ tablespoons honey
¼ cup chilli sauce
2 tablespoons lime juice, freshly squeezed

1. Place the wings and marinade ingredients in a bowl and toss to coat evenly.
2. Cover the bowl and place in fridge to marinate for at least 30 minutes, or overnight. The longer you can do this the more intense the flavour will be. Transfer to the slow cooker.
3. Cook on LOW for 4 hours.

NOTE: Coconut aminos sauce is a soy-free alternative to soy sauce. Once cooked, the pan juices can be thickened with a little cornflour mixed with water, if you like.

Felicity Barnett and Susannah Durbidge

Pork Fillet with Apple & Honey

Pork and apple are a great combination. I wanted to cook my pork fillet slowly so it didn't dry out, and the apple inserted into the pork kept it nice and moist. The honey on top is just gorgeous and you can really taste the apple throughout each slice of the pork. The smell when it's cooking is just lovely, and my children were excited to have fruit included in their dinner and asked for seconds.

Serves 6 • Preparation 10 mins • Cook 4–6 hours • Cooker capacity 6.5 litres

1 onion, thinly sliced
2 Granny Smith apples, thinly sliced
1 pork fillet
Pinch of cinnamon
Drizzle of honey

1. Place the onion and half the apple into the slow cooker. Cut deep slits along the pork fillet and stuff each slit with a halved apple slice.
2. Sit the pork on top of the onion and apple. Sprinkle very lightly with the cinnamon, drizzle with honey and season with salt and pepper.
3. Cover and cook on LOW for 4–6 hours, depending on the thickness of the fillet. When ready it will be tender enough to slice easily, but not to pull apart.

Jamie Murphy

One Pot Chicken Alfredo Pasta

Use any leftover cooked chicken, or grab a BBQ chicken on your way home. This is easy and tasty and kids love to help make this.

Serves 4 • Preparation 20 mins • Cook 3¾ hours • Cooker capacity 6 litres

- 800 ml (27 fl oz) cooking cream
- 375 g (13 oz) block cream cheese, cubed
- 90 g (3 oz) butter, cubed
- ½ cup grated parmesan cheese
- ½ teaspoon garlic powder
- ½ teaspoon onion powder
- Shredded cooked chicken (I used 2 breasts and some meat from the back of the whole chicken)
- 150 g penne pasta
- ½ cup grated parmesan cheese, extra

1. Combine the cream, cream cheese, butter, parmesan, garlic powder and onion powder in the slow cooker. Season with salt and pepper.
2. Cover and cook on LOW for 2 hours 45 minutes, stirring occasionally to break down the cream cheese.
3. Stir in the chicken and pasta. Cover and cook for 1 hour or until pasta is cooked to your liking (time may vary in different slow cookers). Keep an eye on it to make sure it doesn't dry out – additional cream could be added if needed.
4. Stir through extra parmesan then serve immediately.

NOTE: This is a thick creamy coated pasta. If you like a runnier, saucier Alfredo then par-boil the pasta before adding. Cook for only 15 minutes or until the chicken is heated through and pasta is tender. Semi-cooked or cooked pasta won't absorb as much of the sauce as the raw pasta does. The cooking cream is important as it resists splitting like normal cream.

Paulene Christie

Honey Mustard Chicken Wings

Finger licking good! Easy to prepare and slow cook, budget friendly and loved by the whole family!

Serves 4–6 • Preparation 5 mins • Cook 4 hours • Cooker capacity 6 litres

- 1 kg (2 lb 3 oz) chicken wings, tips removed if you prefer
- ½ cup honey
- ⅓ cup mustard (I like mild American mustard)
- 1 tablespoon wholegrain mustard
- ¼ teaspoon paprika
- ¼ teaspoon garlic powder

1. Place the wings into the slow cooker. Combine all the other ingredients and pour over the wings.
2. Cover and cook on LOW for 4 hours.

NOTE: If you are around during cooking time, gently move the wings around in the sauce or baste halfway through cooking to ensure they all get covered in the sauce for rich colour and taste.

Paulene Christie

Sweet & Sour Pork Rashers

This sweet & sour flavour-packed pork rasher recipe was a huge hit with our kids! I served it with brown rice and steamed broccolini for high fives all round!

Serves 5 • Preparation 20 mins • Cook 5 hours • Cooker capacity 6 litres

- 1 kg (2 lb 3 oz) pork rashers
- 1 tablespoon oil
- ½ red capsicum (pepper), sliced
- ½ green capsicum (pepper), sliced
- ¾ cup sugar
- ½ cup salt-reduced soy sauce
- ½ cup white vinegar
- ½ cup canned crushed pineapple
- 2 tablespoons yellow mustard
- 1 heaped teaspoon minced garlic
- 1 heaped teaspoon minced ginger
- Brown rice and steamed broccolini, to serve

1. Cut the pork rashers into thirds. Heat the oil in a frying pan over medium-high heat. Cook the pork rashers for about 5 minutes, turning once, until sealed. Transfer to the slow cooker.
2. Add the capsicum. Combine the remaining ingredients and pour into the slow cooker. Season with salt and pepper.
3. Cover and cook for 4–5 hours on HIGH. Put a tea towel (dish towel) under the lid for the last hour of cooking, which will help to thicken the sauce a little by absorbing excess moisture.
4. Served with brown rice and steamed broccolini

NOTE: I only drizzled a little of the sauce over the finished pork for serving because it's high in sugar, but you could add as much as you like over yours.

Paulene Christie

Easy Tomato Sausages

A chef at our day care centre makes this for the children, and shared the recipe. It is nice and easy and my kids love it. It's a one pot dish with hardly any prep – and who doesn't love sausages!

Serves 6 • Preparation 10 mins • Cook 6–8 hours • Cooker capacity 6 litres

12 sausages
420 g (15 oz) can condensed tomato soup
500 g (1 lb 2 oz) jar pasta sauce
Diced frozen vegetables (optional)
Steamed rice or mashed potato, to serve

1. Combine all the ingredients in the slow cooker.
2. Cover and cook on LOW for 6–8 hours.
3. Cut sausages into smaller pieces, and serve with rice or mashed potato.

Nicole Owens

Citrus Silverside & Vegetables

Our kids love silverside. I wanted a fresh, zesty, sugar-free new way to serve it and this was perfect. Minimal prep means the kids can help with this one also. I've added the option to cook your side vegetables at the same time too, so that busy families could enjoy a fuss-free one-pot dinner, or just the silverside by itself, the choice is yours.

Serves 5 • Preparation 10 mins • Cook 6–7 hours • Cooker capacity 6 litres

1–2 kg (2 lb 3 oz–4 lb 6 oz) piece silverside (or brisket)
1 lime, halved
1 lemon, halved
1.25 L (42 fl oz) sparkling mineral water
Vegetables of choice (optional)

1. Rinse the silverside and place into the slow cooker. Add the lime and lemon, and pour the mineral water over. It's OK if it doesn't completely cover the silverside.
2. Cook on HIGH for 6–7 hours. I turn mine over halfway if I'm home, but I don't worry if I don't.
3. If you want to include the vegetable sides, peel or wash the vegetables and place them into an oven bag. Tie the bag and pierce at the top as per the oven bag instructions to allow venting. Slowly submerge the bag gently into the slow cooker beside your silverside at the desired time remaining (below), leaving the pierced area and tie above water level.

NOTE: Add hard vegetables like potato, carrot or sweet potato 3 hours before the silverside is done. Soft vegetables like zucchini, asparagus or broccoli should be added 1 hour before the silverside is done. You can add multiple bags if they fit. Check vegetable tenderness to be sure they are done to your liking.

Paulene Christie

Beef & Beans Goulash

My boys loved this recipe when they were kids, and were keen to have a go at doing it themselves. This is great on cold days watching the footy on TV!

Serves 4–6 • Preparation 15 mins • Cook 5–6 hours • Cooker capacity 6 litres

500 g (1 lb 2 oz) minced (ground) beef
1 onion, diced
3–4 rashers bacon, diced
1 red or green capsicum (pepper), diced
1 garlic clove, minced (optional)
430 g (15 oz) can condensed tomato soup
½ cup small shell pasta or macaroni
2 tablespoons BBQ sauce
425 g (15 oz) can baked beans
Grated cheese, to serve

1. Brown the beef, onion, capsicum, bacon and garlic together in a frying pan. Transfer to the slow cooker and add the soup, pasta, BBQ sauce and 1 cup water. Stir to combine.
2. Cover and cook on LOW for 5–6 hours. Add baked beans and cook for a further 1 hour.
3. Serve in bowls with grated cheese on top.

Sue McCracken

French Onion Chops

This is a family favourite, and it's so easy to make.

Serves 6 • Preparation 5 mins • Cook 5–6 hours • Cooker capacity 5.5 litre

6 lamb forequarter chops
40 g (1½ oz) packet French onion soup mix
Peas, carrots and mashed potato, to serve

1. Place chops into the slow cooker and sprinkle the soup mix over.
2. Cover and cook on AUTO for 5–6 hours, or 7–8 hours on LOW.
3. Serve with peas, carrots and mashed potato.

Annmarie Fothergill

3 Ingredient Alfredo Chicken & Broccoli

There is nothing plain and boring about chicken and broccoli when you add a cheesy Alfredo sauce. Only 3 ingredients makes for an easy, but tasty, throw-together meal.

Serves 4–6 • Preparation 5 mins • Cook 3–4 hours • Cooker capacity 6 litres

4 chicken breast fillets
490 g (1 lb 2 oz) jar Alfredo sauce
1 head broccoli, cut into florets
Pasta or mashed potato, to serve

1. Place the chicken into the slow cooker.
2. Cover and cook on HIGH for 2½–3 hours, until cooked through.
3. Drain the juices from the slow cooker and add the Alfredo sauce, then the broccoli. Cook for a further 30–45 minutes, depending on how you like your broccoli.
4. Serve with pasta or mashed potato.

Nicole Hansen

Cola Silverside Surprise

My kids love this recipe – they never know which flavour they are going to get.

Serves 6 • Preparation 5 mins • Cook 8–10 hours • Cooker capacity 3.5 litres

2 kg (4 lb 6 oz) piece silverside
2 x 375ml cans cola (or any soft drink you prefer)
Vegetables and gravy, to serve

1. Wash the silverside and place into the slow cooker. Pour the cola over.
2. Cover and cook on LOW for 8–10 hours.
3. Serve with vegetables and gravy.

NOTE: Lemonade is a great alternative to the cola.

Melissa Walden

MINCE & MEATBALLS

Rich Gravy Mince

This budget and family friendly flavoured mince meat is LOVED by our kids. It's so versatile that you can be sure you'll find a way to serve it that your children will love too. Simple ingredients, simple to cook and tastes like old-school meat pie filling!

Serves 6 • Preparation 10 mins • Cook 4 hours • Cooker capacity 6 litres

- 1 kg (2 lb 3 oz) minced (ground) beef
- 2 beef stock cubes, crushed
- 2 onions, finely diced
- ½ cup of your favourite gravy powder

1. Combine all the ingredients in the slow cooker and stir in 1 cup water.
2. Cover and cook on LOW for 4 hours, stirring occasionally if possible to keep the mince separated.
3. Serve on bread rolls as sliders, with vegetables, in pies or on toasted sandwiches.

Paulene Christie

Easy Chow Mein

This is a great budget friendly meal the whole family can enjoy. Mince, vegetables, noodles and egg with a tasty Asian flavour! A fun meal kids enjoy eating and can help cook.

Serves 5 • Preparation 15 mins • Cook 4 hours 35 mins • Cooker capacity 6 litres

1 kg (2 lb 3 oz) minced (ground) beef
2 tablespoons salt-reduced soy sauce
1 heaped teaspoon minced garlic
1 heaped teaspoon minced ginger
1 teaspoon sesame oil
350 g (12½ oz) slaw mix (shredded cabbage, carrot, celery, red onion)
½ cup sliced spring onions (scallions)
2 x 70 g (2⅓ oz) packets instant 2 minute noodles (I use Mi Goreng flavour)
4 eggs

1. Combine the beef mince, soy sauce, garlic, ginger and sesame oil in the slow cooker.
2. Cover and cook on LOW for 4 hours, stirring occasionally to break up any lumps.
3. Add the slaw mix, spring onions and 1 of the flavour sachets from the instant noodle packets Cover and cook on LOW for a further 30 minutes.
4. Towards the end of this time cook the instant noodles as per instructions (but only use the one remaining seasoning packet with the two noodle blocks). When cooked drain the seasoned cooking water and add just the cooked noodles to the slow cooker. After 5 minutes, transfer to serving bowls.
5. Meanwhile, scramble the eggs in a saucepan or frying pan. Alternatively, a fast way to do this is to whisk the eggs and microwave for 3–4 minutes in a large flat bowl until set. Carefully slice or cut up scrambled eggs. Top each serve of chow mein with a few egg strips.

NOTE: Garnish with extra sliced spring onion if you like. You may like to increase the soy sauce or add extra spices (such as chilli), depending on your taste preferences. A sprinkle of curry powder would also be a nice addition. As it is this recipe is mild and friendly for the whole family. It would work equally well with other types of minced meat.

Paulene Christie

Easy Meatballs & Gravy

A fast and easy meatball recipe for the whole family. Kids love getting their hands in and rolling the balls too! You could use chicken mince with chicken gravy, or pork mince with roast pork gravy. Whatever your family likes!

Makes 30 meatballs • Preparation 20 mins • Cook 4 hours • Cooker capacity 6 litres

600 g (1 lb 5 oz) pork and veal mince (see note)
1 egg
½ cup packaged breadcrumbs
2 cups gravy (made with instant gravy powder and cold water)
Spray oil

1. Combine the mince, egg and breadcrumbs with clean hands and roll into small golf ball–sized balls.
2. Spray the slow cooker bowl with oil and add the meatballs. Pour the gravy over.
3. Cover and cook on LOW for 4 hours.

NOTE: Follow packet directions on your gravy powder for how much water to add, to make it up to 2 cups.

Paulene Christie

Carbonara Chicken Meatballs

Easy creamy chicken carbonara meatballs! Perfect to serve on subs, or even just with the vegetables of your choice. Kids can even help you make them!

Makes 20 • Preparation 15 mins • Cook 3 hours • Cooker capacity 6 litres

500 g (1 lb 2 oz) minced (ground) chicken
½ cup panko breadcrumbs
2 teaspoons minced garlic
1 teaspoon dried rosemary
1 teaspoon dried thyme
½ teaspoon cracked black pepper
½ teaspoon salt
500 g (1 lb 2 oz) bottle of your favourite carbonara sauce

1. Combine all the ingredients (except the carbonara sauce) in a large bowl to make the meatballs. Wash your hands and leave them wet as it makes rolling easier and less messy. Roll into 20 small balls about the size of a golf ball.
2. Pour the carbonara sauce into the slow cooker. Gently place the meatballs in the sauce.
3. Cover, putting a tea towel (dish towel) under the lid, and cook on LOW for 3 hours. Do NOT stir or move the meatballs until the last hour to ensure that they are firm. Disturbing them before they are cooked will break them.

Paulene Christie

Creamy Mushroom Meatballs

I looked at the mince and looked at my spices and sauces and thought, 'Yep, this will work'!

Serves 4–6 • Preparation 10 mins • Cook 4 hours • Cooker capacity 5 litres

MEATBALLS
600 g (1 lb 5 oz) minced (ground) beef
⅔ cup breadcrumbs
1 egg
2 tablespoons minced garlic
1 teaspoon dried oregano
1 teaspoon dried thyme
1 teaspoon dried basil

SAUCE
420 g (15 oz) can condensed cream of mushroom soup
300 ml (10 fl oz) cooking cream
40 g (1½ oz) packet French onion soup mix (salt-reduced)
2 tablespoons cream cheese
1 tablespoon Worcestershire sauce

1. Mix all the meatball ingredients together until well combined then roll into small balls. Place into the slow cooker.
2. Mix the sauce ingredients together and pour over the meatballs.
3. Cover and cook on LOW for 4 hours.

NOTE: Serve with brown rice and steamed vegetables, any type of pasta or even mashed potatoes.

Rachel Gerhardy

Spaghetti & Meatballs

This is a great recipe that I'm sure the whole family will love! I love meatballs and I am always trying to improve their texture so they don't fall apart. The kids will absolutely demolish these without hesitation and they won't be able to notice the goodness of the veggies throughout the sauce. It's a great way to get your kids to eat their veggies without them knowing they're actually eating them!

Serves 4–6 • Preparation 20 mins • Cook 5½–6½ hours • Cooker capacity 6 litre

SAUCE
500 g jar (1 lb 2 oz) pasta sauce of your choice
400 g (14 oz) can diced tomatoes
1 carrot, grated
1 zucchini, grated
200 g (7 oz) sliced mushrooms

MEATBALLS
500 g (1 lb 2 oz) lean minced (ground) beef
½–1 cup breadcrumbs
1 onion, diced
1 egg
1 teaspoon dried mixed or Italian herbs
Sprinkle of chopped parsley
Dash each of BBQ and tomato sauce (ketchup)
Spaghetti and grated cheese, to serve

1. To make the sauce, combine all the ingredients in the slow cooker. Cover and turn on HIGH while you make the meatballs.
2. For the meatballs, combine all the ingredients in a mixing bowl and season with salt and pepper. Use your hands to mix well, then roll into small balls. Uncover slow cooker and gently place meatballs into sauce. Do not stir.
3. Cover and cook on HIGH for 1½ hours, then stir the meatballs gently through the sauce (or spoon it over the meatballs). Reduce cooker to LOW and cook a further 4–5 hours.
4. Season sauce with salt and pepper. Serve meatballs and sauce over spaghetti, sprinkled with cheese.

NOTE: The trick to keep the meatballs from falling apart is to not stir them in the first 1½ hours of cooking.

Jenny Small

Mexican Chicken Porcupines

A Mexican chicken version of tomato beef porcupines with a taco twist! Serve with mashed potato and vegetables or on hotdog rolls to make meatball subs. These are great as an easy party food, family meal or picnic lunch.

Makes 28 • Preparation 20 mins • Cook 5 hours • Cooker capacity 6 litres

500 g (1 lb 2 oz) minced (ground) chicken
½ cup long grain white rice, uncooked
1 large onion, grated
1 tablespoon minced garlic
½ teaspoon each salt and pepper
2 x 35 g (1 oz) sachets taco seasoning
½ cup plain (all-purpose) flour, to dust meatballs
400 g (14 oz) can diced tomatoes
2 x 420 g (15 oz) cans cream of tomato soup concentrate

1. Combine the minced chicken, rice, onion, garlic, salt, pepper and 1 tablespoon of taco seasoning in a large bowl. Using clean hands, mix well then form into small balls (about the size of a golf ball).
2. Spread the flour onto a plate. Roll each ball lightly in flour to coat and shake off excess. Set aside.
3. Combine the tomatoes, soup and remaining taco seasoning in the slow cooker. Gently drop the meatballs one at a time into the sauce in a single layer.
4. Cover and cook on LOW for 5 hours. Resist stirring at all until at least halfway through cooking to be sure the meatballs are firm so they don't break apart. When you do stir, just gently move them around in the sauce one or two times (if at all).

Paulene Christie

Meatballs In Tomato Sauce

I had never made these before and was looking for a low-fat recipe which I could make in 10 minutes and just chuck in the slow cooker to cook for a few hours. Most kids like meatballs and it is really easy for them to help make these.

Serves 4 • Preparation 15 mins • Cook 6–8 hours • Cooker capacity 3 litres

500 g (1 lb 2 oz) minced (ground) beef
1 onion, chopped
2 tablespoons thyme leaves
2 teaspoons oregano
1 garlic clove, minced (optional)
Finely chopped chilli, to taste (optional)
2 x 400 g (14 oz) cans chopped tomatoes (try the chopped tomatoes with herbs)
Pasta, to serve

1. Put the mince, onion, thyme, oregano, garlic and chilli into a bowl. Season with salt and pepper, and use hands to mix together. Roll the mixture into 20 small balls.
2. Brown the meatballs in a frying pan then place into the slow cooker. Add the tomatoes and 100 ml (3½ fl oz) water.
3. Cover and cook on LOW for 6–8 hours, stirring halfway through cooking.
4. Serve with pasta.

NOTE: If you are trying to get your children to eat more veggies without them noticing, add some chopped red and green capsicum (pepper) in with the sauce.

Elaine Hunt

Butter Chicken Meatballs

This dish is mild enough for young children to enjoy, but has plenty of flavour for adult tastes! Packed with hidden vegetables too.

Serves 6–8 • Preparation 20 mins • Cook 3–4 hours • Cooker capacity 6 litres

1 carrot, finely grated
1 zucchini, finely grated
500 g (1 lb 2 oz) minced (ground) chicken
½ cup breadcrumbs
2 eggs
1 spring onion (scallion), finely chopped
2 x 400 g (14 oz) cans diced tomatoes
200 g (7 oz) natural yoghurt
⅓ jar mild butter chicken paste

1. Squeeze the excess water from the grated vegetables. Combine in a mixing bowl with the chicken, breadcrumbs, eggs and spring onion. Season with salt and pepper and mix until well combined.
2. Place the tomatoes, yoghurt and butter chicken paste into the slow cooker and stir to combine.
3. Roll the chicken mixture into balls about the size of golf balls. Place into the sauce mixture.
4. Cover and cook on HIGH for 3–4 hours (or LOW 7–8 hours).

Rhiannon Alcock

Tasty Meatloaf with Apple & Leek by Saz

This is the most amazing meatloaf I have ever made. It carves perfectly and is always devoured by my four fussy boys. A simple, tasty winner!

Serves 4–6 • Preparation 20 mins • Cook 6–8 hours • Cooker capacity 6.5 litres

500 g (1 lb 2 oz) sausage meat (I skinned 7 sausages)
250 g (9 oz) lean minced (ground) beef
1 cup breadcrumbs, plus extra for rolling
1 small leek, finely chopped
1 green apple, peeled and grated
1 egg
¼ cup chopped parsley
2 tablespoons wholegrain mustard
2 garlic cloves, finely chopped
Oil, to grease
Mashed potatoes and vegetables or salad, to serve

1. Mix all the ingredients in a large bowl until well combined. Shape into a loaf the length of your slow cooker and roll it in breadcrumbs.
2. Oil the slow cooker and add the meatloaf.
3. Cook on LOW for 6–8 hours.
4. Remove meatloaf from the slow cooker, cover with foil and allow to rest for 20 minutes before carving.
5. Serve with mashed potato and vegetables or a fresh green salad.

NOTE: If you notice a lot of moisture building up, pop a tea towel under the slow cooker lid.

Sarah Atherton

Cheat's Italian Meatballs (With Hidden Veg)

This is easy and tasty and has some sneaky hidden vegetables for those fussy little eaters. The beauty of cooking this in the slow cooker is that the grated vegetables break down and make a lovely rich sauce.

Serves 6 • Preparation 10 mins • Cook 6–8 hours • Cooker capacity 6 litres

8 Italian sausages
1 onion, diced
1 zucchini, grated
1 carrot, grated
400 g (14 oz) can diced tomatoes (or tomato soup)
1 tablespoon minced garlic
1 tablespoon soy sauce
1 teaspoon dried Italian herbs
Spaghetti and shaved parmesan cheese, to serve

1. Cut the sausages in half, squeeze 2 portions out of each and roll into balls. Brown the meatballs in a frying pan and discard excess oil (this is optional – it doesn't really change the taste but it does change the texture of the meatballs).
2. Transfer meatballs to the slow cooker and add the remaining ingredients.
3. Cook on LOW for 6–8 hours.
4. Serve with spaghetti and shaved parmesan.

Fiona Masters

Family-friendly Loaded Mince

This is an easy mince dish that can be as simple as mince served with mashed potato or rice, or you could put mashed potato or sweet potatoes on top to make a shepherd's or cottage pie. It also makes a great filling for a pastry pie.

Serves 6–8 • Preparation 10 mins • Cook 7 hours • Cooker capacity 5.5 litres

- 2 kg (4 lb 6 oz) mince
- 500 g (1 lb 2 oz) bacon, diced
- 2 large tomatoes, diced
- 420 g (15 oz) can corn kernels, drained (or 2½ cups frozen corn)
- 300 g (10½ oz) mushrooms, sliced
- 150 g (5½ oz) spinach, chopped (you can use frozen)
- 3 zucchini or patty pan squash, diced
- 1 tablespoon dried mixed herbs (thyme, oregano, basil)
- Pinch each of salt and cracked pepper
- 2–3 tablespoons golden syrup

1. Place all the ingredients into the slow cooker.
2. Cover and cook on LOW for about 7 hours.

NOTE: Any other vegetables you want can be added – if I don't need to be FODMAP friendly then I add an onion and a handful of garlic cloves. If you can't tolerate mushrooms leave them out. I find the cooking time very forgiving and have left it for 10–11 hours without a problem.

Felicity Barnett

Turkey Meatballs

I originally created this recipe for those following a low-carb way of eating. However, my family decided they loved it too so now we make it for everyone. These can be served with salad, seasonal veggies, pasta or even on subs!

Serves 5 • Preparation 20 mins • Cook 1¾ hours • Cooker capacity 6 litres

500 g (1 lb 2 oz) turkey mince
70 g (2⅓ oz) flax almond baking meal
1 egg
½–1 teaspoon cracked black pepper
½–1 teaspoon all-purpose seasoning
2 teaspoons butter
300 ml (10 fl oz) cooking cream
1 tablespoon minced garlic

1. Combine the turkey mince, almond meal, egg and seasonings in a large mixing bowl. Use your hands to mix well, then roll into 25 balls about the size of a golf ball.
2. Melt the butter in a searing slow cooker or frying pan. Gently add meatballs and cook for 10 minutes, carefully turning once during cooking. Don't worry if they aren't evenly browned all over. Place into the slow cooker.
3. Combine the cooking cream and garlic and pour over the meatballs.
4. Cover, putting a tea towel (dish towel) under the lid, and cook on LOW for 1½ hours.

NOTE: The cooking cream is important as it resists splitting like normal cream.

Paulene Christie

Rissoles in BBQ sauce

This sauce is a fave in our house. I serve the rissoles with creamy mashed potatoes and veggies and drizzle the BBQ sauce over everything, then have leftovers with rice the next day. You can use this sauce in many different dishes. I have used it for chicken, beef chunks, ribs, rissoles, even dim sims.

Serves 4–6 • Preparation 5 minutes • Cook 3–4 or 6–7 hours • Cooker capacity 5–6 litres

6–8 rissoles of your choice

SAUCE
1 cup BBQ sauce
2 tablespoons honey
2 tablespoons tomato sauce (ketchup)
1 tablespoons soy sauce
1 tablespoon garlic powder

1. Place the rissoles into the slow cooker. Mix everything else in a jug with 2 cups water and pour over the rissoles. You may need a little more water, so the rissoles are just covered.
2. Cover and cook on LOW for 6–7 hours or on HIGH for 3–4 hours.

Amy Stevens

Caz's Mince Bowls

This is quite a treat and just something a little different. You can put in whatever you like – and leave out what the kids don't. The kids can get on board and help out as well!

Serves 6 • Preparation 45 mins • Cook 2½ hours • Cooker capacity 5 litres

- 500 g (1 lb 2 oz) premium minced (ground) beef
- 1 onion, diced
- 2 eggs, lightly beaten
- 2 tablespoons tomato sauce (ketchup)
- 2 tablespoons plain (all-purpose) flour, plus extra for moulding
- 200 g (7 oz) diced bacon
- 1 green capsicum (pepper), diced
- 1 small onion, diced
- 1½ cups grated tasty cheese

1. Line the slow cooker with baking paper. Put the mince, onion, eggs, tomato sauce and flour in a large mixing bowl and use your hands to mix thoroughly. Divide into rissole-sized patties and roll in extra flour.
2. Make a well in the centre of each patty to make into a small 'bowl', and arrange in the slow cooker. Combine the bacon, capsicum and onion, and spoon into the mince 'bowls'.
3. Cover and cook on HIGH for about 2 hours. Put cheese onto each 'bowl'. Cover, with a tea towel (dish towel) under the lid, and cook a further 20 minutes, until melted.

NOTE: You can use silicone cupcake moulds for these if you like, and you can add other favourite ingredients to the 'bowls'.

Carol Wilkinson

Pizza Sloppy Joes

I came up with this recipe when making the original sloppy joes. I wanted to add more veggies and make it a bit more exciting. Why not pizza inspired? This is a great way to add veggies into your family's meal.

Serves 6–8 • Preparation 5 mins • Cook 4 hours • Cooker capacity 5 litres

500 g (1 lb 2 oz) minced (ground) beef
1 brown onion, diced
2 teaspoons minced garlic
500 g (1 lb 2 oz) jar pasta sauce of your choice
1 tablespoon oregano (dried, or chopped fresh)
1 tablespoon basil (dried, or chopped fresh)
4–5 mushrooms, diced
Handful of chopped pepperoni
½ red or green capsicum (pepper), diced
Bread rolls and grated tasty cheese, to serve

1. Place all the ingredients into the slow cooker and season with salt and pepper. Mix well.
2. Cook on LOW for 4 hours.
3. Serve on bread rolls, sprinkled with cheese.

NOTE: If it is too runny mix through some cornflour mixed with water to thicken.

Tara Beynon

BIRTHDAY PARTY

Cob-less Hot Cob Dip

Think of a lush cob loaf – minus the cob! Our kids love to tuck into this at parties with carrot, cucumber and celery sticks, bread sticks, or tortilla chips. It's great for low-carb folk, for parties and entertaining. A cheesy, creamy dip delight!

Serves 10 • Preparation 15 mins • Cook 1¾ hours • Cooker capacity 6 litres

- 250 g (9 oz) block cream cheese, chopped
- ⅔ cup cooking cream
- ⅔ cup sour cream
- 150 g (5½ oz) diced bacon
- 1 cup grated tasty cheese
- 40 g (1½ oz) packet French onion soup mix
- ¼ cup chopped fresh chives
- ⅔ cup grated mozzarella cheese

1. Lay a sheet of baking paper on the base of the slow cooker bowl (just to protect the surface). Pour enough water into the bowl so it is 2 cm (¾ inch) deep. Sit a suitably sized (heatproof) serving dish into the water bath in the slow cooker.
2. Combine the cream cheese, cream, sour cream, bacon, tasty cheese and soup mix in a mixing bowl. Mix well, then transfer to the serving dish.
3. Cover, putting a tea towel (dish towel) under the lid, and cook on HIGH for 1½ hours, stirring once during cooking time.
4. Sprinkle top with the chives and mozzarella cheese, cover (replace the tea towel) and cook for a further 15 minutes.
5. Carefully remove the dish from the slow cooker. Wipe the water from the bottom of the dish then serve straight to the table.

NOTE: I used an ovenproof ceramic dish about 23 cm (9 inches) long, 15 cm (6 inches) wide and 7cm (2¾ inches) deep.

Paulene Christie

Caz's Easy Peasy Kebabs

This recipe is just so popular and easy to make. You can prepare everything then get the kids involved with making their own kebabs. That way they don't have to pick off what they don't want!

Makes 12–18 • Preparation 30 mins • Cook 1–1½ hours • Capacity 5 litres

Oil, for greasing
6 thin sausages, thickly sliced
500 g (1 lb 2 oz) kabana (about 6), thickly sliced
2 chicken breasts, cubed
3 tomatoes, chopped
2 x 440 g (15½ oz) cans pineapple chunks, drained
2 onions, cut into large chunks
2 green capsicums (peppers), cut into large chunks

1. Soak wooden skewers in water for 20 minutes. Grease the slow cooker with oil. Thread the ingredients onto the skewers. If you like, brown them in a little oil in a frying pan before adding to the slow cooker. Arrange in a single layer in the slow cooker.
2. Cover, putting a tea towel (dish towel) under the lid, and cook on HIGH for 1–1½ hours (depending on your slow cooker).

Carol Wilkinson

Coconut Cake or Donuts

My daughter wanted donuts and coconut cake for her birthday, and after a day of baking on the weekend we had both.

Makes 1 cake or 12 donuts • Preparation 5 mins • Cook 2–4½ hours
• Cooker capacity 7 litres

- 1 cup self-raising flour (or gluten-free self-raising flour)
- 1 cup coconut sugar or brown sugar
- 1 cup desiccated coconut
- 1 cup coconut milk

1. Combine all the dry ingredients in a mixing bowl. Add the coconut milk and stir until combined. Pour into a greased and lined cake tin or greased donut trays or muffin tins.
2. Place tin on a rack in the slow cooker, with about 2.5 cm (1 inch) of water in the base.
3. Cover, putting a tea towel (dish towel) under the lid, and cook on HIGH for 4–4½ hours for a cake tin, or 2–2½ hours for donut trays or muffin tins. Cake is cooked when a skewer inserted into the centre comes out clean.

NOTE: The cooking time may vary depending on the flour used and on your slow cooker. For a chocolate variation, add 1 or 2 tablespoons of cocoa powder with the dry ingredients. For a quick simple icing we mix leftover coconut milk with some pure icing sugar and drizzle over cake once cooled.

Felicity Barnett and Susannah Durbidge

Chocolate Spiders

Chocolate spiders are fun and yummy for kids and adults. We make them without peanut butter because of allergies and they are a huge hit. It's a quick and easy recipe which is a bonus!

Makes 12 • Preparation 5 mins • Cook 20 mins • Cooker capacity 5 litres

200 g (7 oz) chocolate (milk or dark)
2 tablespoons crunchy peanut butter (optional)
1 teaspoon butter (if leaving out peanut butter)
100 g (3½ oz) packet fried noodles

1. Turn slow cooker onto HIGH. Place chocolate and peanut butter (or butter if not using peanut butter) into slow cooker with the lid off.
2. Stir every 5–10 minutes, until melted and combined. Add noodles and stir until well coated.
3. Line a tray with baking paper and drop tablespoons of mixture onto it. Refrigerate until firm.

Kylie de Koning

Mexican Pulled Pork Sliders

Saucy pulled pork – great for parties and entertaining. It's easy to serve on sliders with a fresh crunchy slaw and if your kids are anything like mine they love any dinner on bread rolls! With only 3 ingredients, this is simple enough for the kids to make under your supervision.

Serves 10–12 • Preparation 10 mins • Cook 9 hours • Cooker capacity 6 litres

1.5 kg (3 lb 5 oz) piece boneless pork
400 g (14 oz) can diced tomatoes
2 x 30 g (1 oz) packets reduced-salt taco seasoning
Bread rolls and crunchy slaw, to serve

1. Leave the fat on the pork and place fat side down into slow cooker. Pour the tomatoes over and sprinkle with the seasoning.
2. Cover and cook on LOW for 9 hours.
3. Carefully turn the pork over. Remove and discard the fat layer. Use plastic utensils or tongs (to protect your cooker) to shred and pull the pork into the cooking liquid.
4. Serve on bread rolls with crunchy slaw. Great for guests to self serve at parties too!

NOTE: I prefer the salt-reduced taco mix but you could use regular.

Paulene Christie

Cheesy Chilli Dogs

A sure fire hit with the kids!! These are also great for party food at your next fun occasion. Take hot dogs to the NEXT LEVEL with this American inspired hotdog dish! This recipe will make enough chilli to top up to 24 hotdogs, so use what you want and freeze leftovers for an easy dinner in the future.

Makes up to 24 hotdogs • Preparation 10 mins • Cook 5 hours • Cooker capacity 6 litres

1 kg (2 lb 3 oz) minced (ground) beef
⅔ cup beef stock
1 cup passata (puréed tomato)
140 g (5 oz) can tomato paste (concentrated purée)
⅓ cup tomato sauce (ketchup)
2 tablespoons Worcestershire sauce
2 teaspoons ground chilli
1 teaspoon onion powder

TO SERVE
Hot dogs, heated
Hot dog buns, split
Grated tasty cheese

1. Combine the mince and stock in the slow cooker. Using a plastic potato masher (so you don't scratch the bowl), mash the two together. This makes a nice fine mince in your final dish to serve on your hot dogs. If you don't have a plastic potato masher, do this step in another dish then add to the slow cooker.
2. Add the remaining ingredients to your slow cooker and stir well to combine.
3. Cover and cook on LOW for 5 hours, then pour the mixture through a fine strainer to remove the liquid and leave you with just the chilli meat.
4. To serve, place the hot dogs into the buns and top with 2–3 tablespoons of chilli each. Sprinkle generously with grated cheese

NOTE: While the chilli in the slow cooker had some heat to it, once drained of liquid I found it suitable for our children and only mildly spicy. If you are concerned, though, you could always reduce your chilli powder to 1½ teaspoons.

Paulene Christie

Mini M&M's LCMs

I started making this recipe because my daughter didn't like the shop bought LCMs but when I made these she was very happy to take them to school with her. I like this recipe because it is very easy to change around, which is great with kids' changing favourites. I came up with this recipe purely by putting together all the ingredients my daughter liked into a bar for play lunches.

Makes 20+ • Preparation 3 mins • Cook 30 mins • Cooker capacity 5 litres

125 g (4½ oz) butter
250 g (9 oz) marshmallows
2½ cups chocolate puffed rice cereal
2½ cups puffed rice cereal
¼ cup mini M&M's

1. Line a slice pan with baking paper. Combine the butter and marshmallows in the slow cooker, leaving the lid off.
2. Cook on LOW for 30 minutes, stirring every 5 minutes until melted and combined.
3. Stir in the puffed rice and chocolate puffed rice. Add most of the M&M's and stir gently until mixed through. Turn out into the prepared pan and sprinkle the remaining M&M's on top. Press to smooth the surface.
4. Refrigerate until firm, then cut into bars.

Cheryle Baird

Marshmallow Monsters

This is a kids' snack that's as much fun to create as it is to eat!

Serves 6 • Preparation 10 mins • Cook 40 mins • Cooker capacity 6.5 litres

Spray oil
60 g (2 oz) butter
280 g (10 oz) marshmallows
Green food colouring
6 cups puffed rice cereal
½ cup dark choc melts
12 pretzel sticks (broken in half)
24 candy eyes (or other small round candies)
Red writing icing

1. Grease a 23 cm (9 inch) tray and line with baking paper. Spray the paper with oil. Place the butter and marshmallows into the slow cooker.
2. Cover and cook on HIGH for about 40 minutes, stirring occasionally, until all melted with no lumps.
3. Add green colouring as required until you get the colour you like, mixing until combined. Turn off slow cooker and mix in the puffed rice gently.
4. Pour mixture over prepared tray and using wet hands pat the mixture firmly, smoothing the surface. Place into the fridge to cool and firmly set. Cut into rectangular bars.
5. Line a large tray with baking paper. Place the choc melts in a small bowl and microwave for 40 seconds. Stir and repeat until melted. Allow to cool for 2 minutes. Dip one end of each bar in the melted chocolate and move back and forth for good coverage, to make 'hair'. Shake off excess chocolate, and lay the bar on baking paper. Repeat with remaining bars and chocolate. Push a pretzel half in each side to make arms.
6. Dab a little of the melted chocolate on the back of the candy eyes and place onto the bars. Use red writing icing to pipe mouths onto the monsters. Leave to set.

Denise Roberts

BBQ Bacon Burgers

A tasty BBQ and bacon flavoured filling for burgers or sliders! So easy to make and serve, and inexpensive too. This is a great self serve option for your next party, and if your child is like mine and loves baked beans, they'll LOVE this recipe!

Serves 8–10 • Preparation 15 mins • Cook 5 hours • Cooker capacity 6 litres

1 kg (2 lb 3 oz) minced (ground) beef
440 g (15½ oz) can baked beans in BBQ sauce
250 g (9 oz) diced bacon
1 cup sugar-free BBQ sauce
1 large onion, diced
1 tablespoon minced garlic
Bread rolls, grated cheese and salad (optional), to serve

1. Combine all the ingredients in the slow cooker and stir well.
2. Cover and cook on LOW for 5 hours.
3. Serve on bread rolls with grated cheese, and salad if you like.

NOTE: Use any leftovers to create a second meal – very versatile!

Paulene Christie

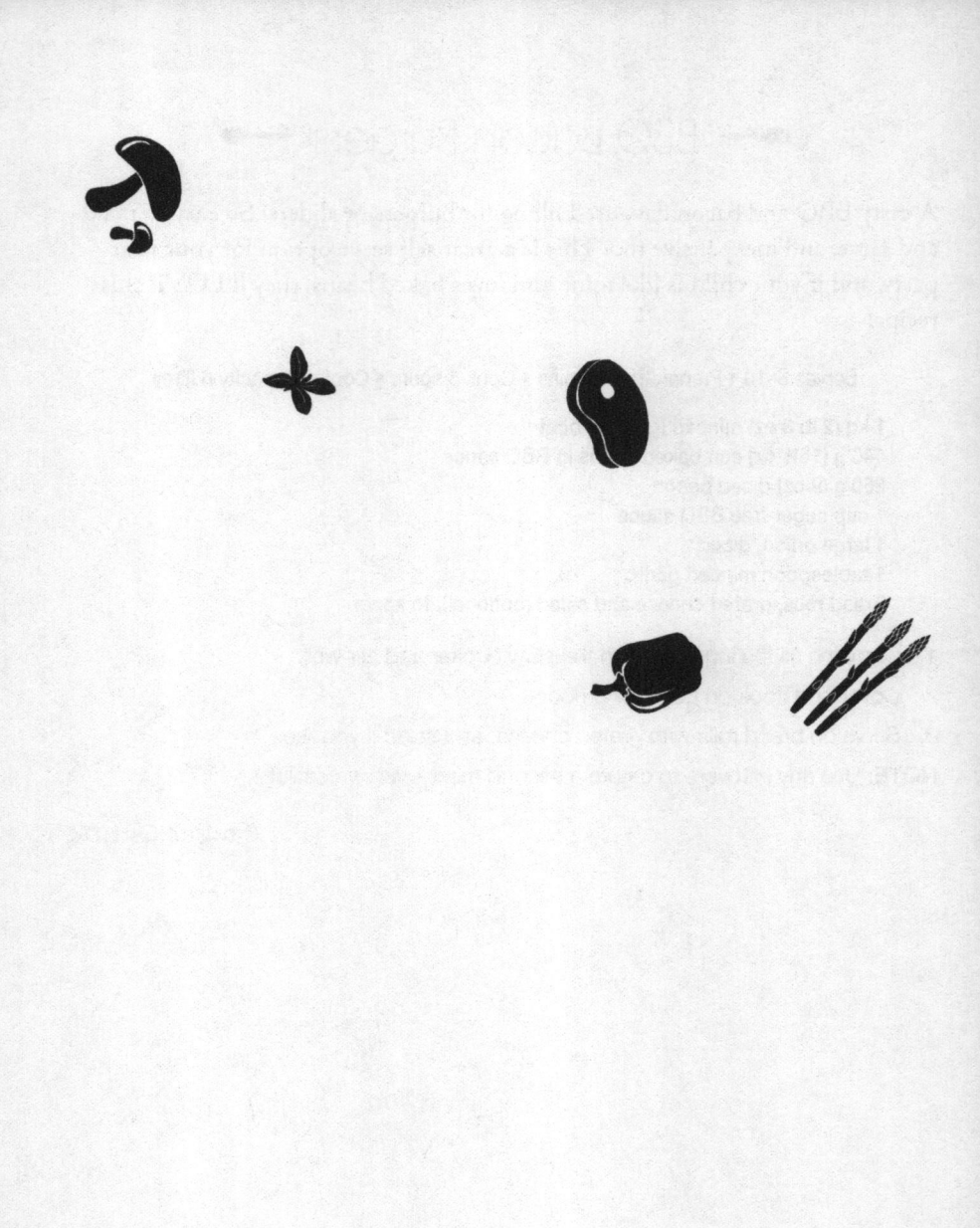

A LITTLE BIT FANCY

Hungarian Chicken

This is an adaptation of a stovetop meal for my slow cooker.

Serves 4–6 • Preparation 15 mins • Cook 5–6 hours • Cooker capacity 3.5 litres

½ cup plain (all-purpose) flour
4 tablespoons paprika
2 tablespoons oil
1–1.5 kg (2 lb 3 oz–3 lb 5 oz) skinless chicken thigh fillets, halved
2 medium onions, sliced
4 garlic cloves, minced
4 large tomatoes, diced (about 2 cups)
1 cup chicken stock
2 tablespoons tomato paste (concentrated purée)
1 tablespoon brown sugar
½ cup sour cream
2 tablespoons cornflour (cornstarch)

1. Mix the flour and 2 tablespoons of the paprika together on a plate. Heat 1 tablespoon of the oil in a frying pan over medium heat.
2. Coat the chicken in the flour mixture and shake off the excess. Cook the chicken in batches until brown both sides (make sure the heat isn't too high or the paprika will burn.) Place chicken into the slow cooker.
3. Heat remaining oil in the pan. Coat the onion in any remaining flour and gently cook the onion and garlic until it is starting to soften. Place into the slow cooker. Add the remaining paprika, the tomatoes, stock, tomato paste and sugar and mix together.
4. Cover and cook on LOW for 5–6 hours.
5. About 10 minutes before serving, mix the sour cream and cornflour in a bowl. Add 3–4 tablespoons of the cooking liquid to this and mix until smooth. Add to the slow cooker, stir through and turn the cooker off (adding a little of the hot liquid to the sour cream mixture before adding it to the dish will help stop it splitting). Season with salt and pepper to taste.

NOTE: This is traditionally made with Hungarian paprika, which is a sweet paprika, so in the absence of that in my cupboard, I used brown sugar to add a little sweetness.

Nikki Willis

Greek Style Lemon & Herb Lamb Leg

This Greek-inspired slow cooked lamb leg is so tender it falls off the bone!

Serves 6–8 • Preparation 10 mins • Cook 10 hours • Cooker capacity 6 litres

- 1 bunch flat-leaf parsley, leaves picked
- ½ cup fresh oregano leaves (or 3 tablespoons dried)
- ¼ cup fresh rosemary leaves (or 1½ tablespoons dried)
- ⅓ cup olive oil
- 6 garlic cloves
- 1 tablespoon salt
- 1 tablespoon black peppercorns
- 2 red onions, sliced
- 2 lemons, sliced
- 2–2.5 kg leg of lamb (shoulder also suits)

1. Blend the herbs, olive oil, garlic, salt and pepper until a pesto-like paste has formed.
2. Line the bottom of the slow cooker with the onions and half the lemon slices. Score the lamb leg deeply on both sides. Rub the herb blend all over the lamb, and place into the slow cooker on top of the onion and lemon. Place the remaining lemon slices on top.
3. Cover and cook on LOW for 8–10 hours, depending on size of leg. I cooked a 2.3 kg leg for 10 hours.
4. Strain the juices from the bottom of the cooker for a delicious gravy!

Emily Furlong

Sweet Orange Silverside

I love using the slow cooker and I love meals that are easy to prepare. My sister-in-law adds oranges to her silverside recipe and always cooks one at Christmas time, so I played with the ingredients to suit me. The citrus flavour comes from oranges, with some sweetness from the brown sugar and a little bit of malty acidity from the balsamic vinegar. The little hints of spice from the cloves and bay leaf make it complete.

Serves 4–6 • Preparation 15 mins • Cook 8–9 hours • Cooker capacity 5–7 litres

500 g–1 kg (1 lb 2 oz–2 lb 3 oz) piece silverside (can be any size as long as it fits comfortably in slow cooker)
4–5 potatoes, halved
2–3 carrots, halved and quartered
1–2 onions, quartered
1–2 oranges, quartered
2 heaped tablespoons brown sugar
6 cloves
2 bay leaves
4 cups vegetable stock
¾ cup balsamic vinegar
Mustard sauce, to serve

1. Place silverside into the slow cooker. Arrange the vegetables and oranges around the meat and add the brown sugar, cloves and bay leaves. Pour the stock and balsamic vinegar over.
2. Cover and cook on LOW for 8–9 hours.
3. Slice and serve with mustard sauce if desired.

NOTE: If you have a smaller slow cooker you can leave out the carrots and potatoes, and decrease the stock to 2 cups.

Sylvia Hillas

A Little Bit Fancy

Spanish Chicken

This recipe may be more suited to the older children and adults of the house. For the little people in our house we just left the chorizo and olives off their plates when serving and they still were able to enjoy this dish with the family. It's also a great low-carb recipe for anyone watching their carb intake.

Serves 6 • Preparation 20 mins • Cook 5½ hours • Cooker capacity 6 litres

2 teaspoons olive oil
1 chorizo sausage, halved lengthways then sliced
1 red onion, sliced
1.5 kg (3 lb 5 oz) chicken drumsticks
400 g (14 oz) can cherry tomatoes in juice
1 red capsicum (pepper), sliced
½ cup chicken stock
2 teaspoons smoked paprika
100 g (3½ oz) mixed green and black pitted olives
Couscous, to serve

1. Sear the chorizo and onion in the olive oil in a searing slow cooker or frying pan for 5–10 minutes or until golden brown. Combine in the slow cooker with all the ingredients except the olives.
2. Cover and cook on LOW for 5 hours.
3. Add the olives and cook for a further 30 minutes. Serve with couscous

Paulene Christie

Nanny's Braised Steak

Melt in your mouth, tender steak in a gravy that will make you literally want to lick your plate! My mum used to make this on the stove for me when I was a child. We lost our mum when we were quite young, so this is a recipe I hold very dear as it always takes me back to that time. The fact that the grandchildren she never met now help me prepare and LOVE to eat 'Nanny's recipe' makes me very proud. I know she would be bursting with pride to see her recipe in this book for everyone to enjoy! This one's for you Mum. xx

Serves 5 • Preparation 15 mins • Cook 5 hours • Cooker capacity 6 litres

- ¼ cup mild American mustard
- ¼ cup brown sugar
- 1 kg (2 lb 3 oz) oyster blade steak (or any affordable casserole-style steak)
- 2 heaped tablespoons plain (all-purpose) flour
- 1 large onion, thinly sliced
- ½ cup tomato sauce (ketchup) (I use low sugar but you can use regular)
- 1½ tablespoons soy sauce (I use salt-reduced but you can use regular)
- Mashed potato and vegetables, to serve

1. Combine the mustard and sugar in a freezer bag. Add the steaks to the bag. Toss and rub around to coat the steaks with the mixture.
2. Place the flour into another freezer bag and season with salt and pepper. Tip the steak from the first bag into the second bag and toss around to dust them with the flour.
3. Remove steaks from the bag and place them in a single layer in the slow cooker. Top with the onion, then combine the sauces and pour over the steaks.
4. Cover and cook on LOW for 5 hours.
5. Serve steak with mashed potato and vegetables, and pour over the lush gravy.

NOTE: You do not need to add any water to this dish, but you could add ½ cup water for extra gravy volume if you like.

Paulene Christie

Chop Suey

This recipe is similar to Mince Chow Mien. My family absolutely love both of these meals. They are full of hidden vegetables that we all enjoy.

Serves 6–8 • Preparation time 30 mins • Cook 5–7 hours • Cooker capacity 6 litres

- 1 tablespoon olive oil
- 1 kg (2 lb 3 oz) minced (ground) beef
- 1 large onion, diced
- 2 mushrooms, diced
- ½ red capsicum (pepper), diced
- ½ green capsicum (pepper), diced
- 2 carrots, grated
- 2 zucchini, grated
- 2 yellow squash, grated
- 2 celery stalks, sliced
- ½ cabbage, shredded
- 3 large spinach leaves, shredded
- 2 x 45 g (1½ oz) packets chicken noodle soup mix
- 2–3 tablespoons curry powder
- 1 tablespoon soy sauce

1. Heat the oil in a large frying pan and cook the mince and onion until brown, breaking up lumps with a wooden spoon as it cooks.
2. Add to the slow cooker with all the vegetables. Combine the soup mix and curry powder and sprinkle over the top. Drizzle with soy sauce and ½ cup water and mix through.
3. Cover and cook on LOW for 5–7 hours.

NOTE: Serve with your choice of steamed rice and pappadams and enjoy.

Judith Clark

Slow Cooked Duck & Veggies

I was looking for a new way to cook duck and came across this recipe which I adapted to suit my family.

Serves 4–6 • Preparation 10 mins • Cook 5 hours • Cooker capacity 5 litres

- 4 large potatoes, peeled and chopped into chunks
- 2 large carrots, peeled and chopped into chunks
- 1 medium onion, coarsely chopped
- 2 tablespoons butter
- 40 g (1½ oz) packet French onion soup mix
- 2 teaspoons chicken stock powder
- 2 ducks
- 1 tablespoon cornflour (cornstarch), if required

1. Place the vegetables, butter, soup mix, stock powder and 1 cup water into the slow cooker and stir to combine. Place ducks on top.
2. Cover and cook on HIGH for 5 hours.
3. Lift the ducks from the slow cooker and slice the meat. If you want to thicken the sauce, mix the cornflour and 2 tablespoons water in a small bowl until smooth. Stir into the sauce to thicken. Season with salt and pepper. Serve duck with the veggies and sauce.

NOTE: You could use other veggies such as pumpkin or sweet potato. I added ready-cooked peas and corn for serving but they could be added in during cooking time.

Nikki Willis

Creamy Cauliflower & Prosciutto Soup

Don't tell the kids this soup is based on cauliflower and they'll never know! Tasty, creamy and perfect served with a crusty bread roll on the side, or as an entrée for a dinner party.

Serves 4–6 • Preparation 15 mins • Cook 5 hours • Cooker capacity 6 litres

- 4 cups vegetable stock (salt-reduced if you prefer)
- 500 g (1 lb 2 oz) cauliflower florets, chopped
- 250 g (9 oz) block cream cheese, cubed
- 1 heaped tablespoon Dijon mustard
- 2 teaspoons butter
- 100 g (3½ oz) prosciutto, cut into short strips

1. Place the stock, cauliflower, cream cheese and mustard into the slow cooker.
2. Cover and cook on LOW for 3 hours.
3. When the soup is almost ready, melt the butter in a frying pan and cook the prosciutto until crisp. Reserve a small amount of the crisp prosciutto to garnish.
4. Using a stick blender, blend the soup until smooth. Add the prosciutto to the soup, stir to combine and continue to cook on LOW for a further 2 hours, for depth of flavour.
5. Serve soup scattered with reserved prosciutto.

NOTE: I blended the soup in a bowl to preserve the surface of my slow cooker then returned it to the slow cooker once blended. The prosciutto could be fried as step 1 in a searing slow cooker if you prefer not to dirty an extra pan, then set aside in fridge until needed. You may prefer to add your prosciutto to soup as is without cooking – that's OK too.

Paulene Christie

Chicken Cordon Bleu Casserole

I love chicken cordon bleu but find it so messy and fiddly to make. So I decided to just throw everything together in the slow cooker and see what happened – the result was amazing and this is now a weekly family favourite!

Serves 4 • Preparation 10 mins • Cook 4–5 hours • Cooker capacity 4.5 litres

400 g (15 oz) can cream of chicken soup (cream of mushroom works well too)
¼ cup milk
½ teaspoon dried oregano
¼ teaspoon garlic powder
¼ teaspoon salt
¼ teaspoon ground black pepper
4 large chicken breast fillets
6 thick slices ham
6 slices Swiss cheese (or 2 cups grated cheddar)
1 cup dry stuffing mix (I used sage and onion)
80 g (2 ¾ oz) butter, melted

1. Whisk the chicken soup, milk, oregano, garlic powder, salt and pepper in a jug until smooth.
2. Arrange the chicken in the bottom of the slow cooker so that the pieces are not overlapping. Layer the ham evenly on top of the chicken, then do the same with the cheese.
3. Pour the soup mixture over and use a spatula to spread out evenly. Sprinkle over some stuffing mix, enough to roughly cover the surface, then drizzle the melted butter all over.
4. Cover and cook on LOW for 4–5 hours undisturbed – don't be tempted to lift the lid and peek!

NOTE: To make this extra cheesy add a good sprinkling of cheese sauce mix to the soup mixture.

Rachel Duncan

Garlic Prawn or Chicken Skewers

These lush garlic butter coated prawn or chicken skewers wrapped in prosciutto are perfect with a side salad for a steamy summer night dinner. They are also great as an entrée, or for entertaining! If your children are helping you to make these, be sure to supervise the threading stage to keep little fingers safe.

Makes 8 • Preparation 30 mins • Cook 15 or 45 mins • Cooker capacity 6 litres

- 8 large green prawns (shrimp), peeled and deveined, or chicken tenderloin strips
- 8 thin slices prosciutto
- 85 g (3 oz) soft garlic butter (or blend your own butter with minced garlic)

1. Soak wooden skewers in water for 15 minutes. Lay out one slice of prosciutto and spread generously with garlic butter. Lay a prawn or chicken strip on the end of the prosciutto and wind until wrapped. Thread onto a skewer. Repeat with remaining ingredients.
2. Line the slow cooker with baking paper. Lay the skewers onto the paper.
3. Cover and cook on HIGH. It will take 15 minutes for prawns or 45 minutes for chicken.
4. If you like, spoon the garlic butter cooking juices over the skewers to serve.

Paulene Christie

Black Bean Quesadillas

This is a family favourite that my son requests all the time. You can add pulled pork or any meat if you choose.

Serves 6+ • Preparation 5 mins • Cook 4 hours • Cooker capacity 5.5 litres

420 g (15 oz) can black beans, rinsed and drained
420 g (15 oz) can corn kernels, drained
300 g (10½ oz) jar salsa
1 onion, diced
30 g (1 oz) packet taco seasoning
1 teaspoon minced garlic
1 cup cooked rice
½ cup grated tasty cheese, plus more for topping
2 tablespoons sour cream
8 wraps
400 g (14 oz) jar pasta sauce

1. Combine the beans, corn, salsa, onion, taco seasoning and garlic in the slow cooker.
2. Cover and cook on LOW for 4 hours.
3. Stir in the rice, cheese and sour cream. Allow to cool if you have time. Preheat oven to 180°C (350°F).
4. Divide the mixture between the wraps. Roll up to enclose the filling and arrange in a single layer in an oven dish. Spoon pasta sauce over and sprinkle with extra cheese. Bake for 15 minutes or until cheese is melted and golden brown.

Katherine Barron

Creamy Paprika Pork

A lovely dish with a smoky taste from the paprika. It's nice and creamy, and great served over pasta.

Serves 6 • Preparation 10 mins • Cook 5–6 hours • Cooker capacity 5.5 litre

1 tablespoon olive oil
1 kg (2 lb 3 oz) diced pork
2 onions, sliced
300 g (10½ oz) sliced mushrooms
250 ml (9 fl oz) chicken stock
5 tablespoons tomato paste (concentrated purée)
3 tablespoons smoked paprika
¼ cup cornflour (cornstarch)
⅓ cup sour cream
Cooked pasta, to serve

1. Heat the oil in a pan and brown the pork and onions, then add to slow cooker.
2. Add the mushrooms, chicken stock, tomato paste and paprika.
3. Cover and cook on LOW for 5–6 hours.
4. If the sauce is too runny, mix the cornflour with ¼ cup water in a small bowl until smooth. Stir into the sauce to thicken.
5. Stir in sour cream, and serve over your favourite pasta.

Lynda Eagleson

Ratatouille

After watching the movie *Ratatouille* for the 15th time, I got to thinking how I could recreate the dish. I came up with this idea with the help of my kids.

Serves 4–8 • Preparation 15 mins • Cook 4–6 hours • Cooker capacity 5 litres

2 x 400 g (14 oz) cans diced tomatoes
2 teaspoons minced garlic
1 teaspoon dried Italian herbs
1 teaspoon smoked paprika
1 zucchini, thinly sliced
2 large potatoes, thinly sliced
1 sweet potato, thinly sliced
1 large onion, quartered
1 cup grated tasty cheese (optional)

1. Mix the tomatoes, garlic, herbs and paprika and season with freshly ground black pepper. Pour half of the mixture into the slow cooker.
2. Layer all the veggies evenly around the edge of the slow cooker. Pour over remaining sauce.
3. Cover and cook on HIGH for 4–6 hours. 1 hour before the end of cooking, sprinkle with the grated cheese, if using.

NOTE: You can use almost any vegetable in this, add a bit of spice to the sauce or even add some bacon in between the slices of veggies.

Lisa Casey

Caz's Chicken Base Pizza

This is a fantastic recipe. I came up with it because one day I had no flour to make a pizza base – and it turned out to be perfect! Great with a side salad.

Serves 4 • Preparation 30 mins • Cook 2–3 hours • Cooker capacity 5 litres

- 1 tablespoon olive oil
- 2 large chicken breast fillets, halved horizontally
- 2 cups passata (puréed tomato)
- 1 onion, sliced
- 1 green capsicum (pepper), sliced
- 200 g (7 oz) bacon, diced
- ½ teaspoon dried oregano
- 2 cups grated tasty cheese

1. Line the slow cooker with baking paper and rub the paper with the oil. Place the chicken between freezer bags and either roll out with a rolling pin or pound gently with a meat mallet.
2. Place into the slow cooker. Press out and shape evenly over the base. Spread with passata then top with onion, capsicum and bacon. Sprinkle with oregano, then 1 cup of the cheese.
3. Cover, putting a tea towel (dish towel) under the lid, and cook on HIGH for 2–3 hours. 15 minutes before the end of cooking time, sprinkle with the remaining cheese.

NOTE: As all slow cookers are different, just check halfway through (some cook quicker or slower than others).

Carol Wilkinson

Jodie's Awesome Roast Pork

We wanted to add more flavour to our roast pork and we did!

Serves 6+ • Preparation 5 mins • Cook 5¼ hours • Cooker capacity – 7 litres

150 ml (5 fl oz) smoky BBQ sauce
⅓ cup honey
¼ cup Worcestershire sauce
2 teaspoons minced garlic
2.5 kg (2 ½ lb) pork shoulder roast, bone in
2-3 tablespoons gravy powder (to your taste)
Roasted vegetables and garlic bread, to serve

1. Place the BBQ sauce, honey, Worcestershire sauce, garlic and ¼ cup water into the slow cooker and mix well. Pat pork dry with paper towel and add to the slow cooker. Turn to coat in the sauce.
2. Cover and cook on HIGH for 2¼ hours then turn to LOW and cook for a further 3 hours (alternatively cook on LOW for 7½ hours). Baste meat with sauce every hour if desired.
3. Remove pork from slow cooker and place onto a board. Cover with foil and let rest for 10 minutes while preparing gravy.
4. Strain the sauce from the slow cooker into a saucepan. Place over medium–low heat, add 1 cup water and 2-3 tablespoons gravy powder and whisk until thickened.
5. Serve with your favourite roasted vegetables and garlic bread.

NOTE: If you fancy pork crackling with this dish, remove the skin before cooking, place it on an oven tray, oil and salt it, then cook it in a pre-heated VERY hot oven until it crackles. Some do this under a grill instead of in the oven, but it needs to be watched closely to ensure it doesn't burn.

Jodie Leemhuis

Caramelised Onion BBQ Ribs

Caramelised onion is a favourite in our household and my husband loves BBQ sauce so thought I'd try my luck and throw them together. The combination of the flavours worked well for a tasty dish.

Serves 4 • Preparation 15 mins • Cook 6–8 hours • Cooker capacity 5 litres

2 teaspoons olive oil
2 brown onions, diced
¼ cup balsamic vinegar
1½ tablespoons brown sugar
8 (about 1 kg/2 lb 3 oz) beef spare ribs
200 g (7 oz) diced bacon
¼ cup BBQ sauce
Steamed rice and vegetables, to serve

1. Heat the oil in a frying pan and cook the onion until golden. Add the vinegar and sugar and bring to a simmer. Cook until most of the balsamic has evaporated.
2. Transfer to the slow cooker and add the ribs, bacon and sauce. Mix so that all the ingredients are covered with sauce.
3. Cover and cook on LOW for 6–8 hours depending on your slow cooker. Serve over rice with vegetables.

NOTE: If time is an issue, add a jar of caramelised onion instead of the onion mixture.

Kelly Joyce

Chicken with Camembert Sauce

This creamy, succulent camembert sauce will have you licking your fingers and begging for more.

Serves 4 • Preparation 10 mins • Cook 4 hours • Cooker capacity 5.5 litres

1½ tablespoons cornflour (cornstarch)
300 ml (10 fl oz) cooking cream
1 large camembert or triple cream brie (about 250 g/9 oz)
4 chicken breast fillets
4 slices bacon, diced (optional)
1 tablespoon sliced almonds (optional)
1 teaspoon minced garlic (optional)

1. Mix the cornflour and ¼ cup of the cream in a small bowl until smooth. Set aside.
2. Remove the skin from the camembert and chop up the inside part (large chunks are fine). Discard the skin. Combine all the ingredients in the slow cooker.
3. Cover and cook on LOW for 4 hours, stirring occasionally.

Denise Roberts

Camembert & Basil Breast Pockets

Enjoy beautiful, succulent slow cooked chicken breasts, stuffed with a creamy camembert and basil filling.

Serves 5 • Preparation 10 mins • Cook 2½ hours • Cooker capacity 6 litres

- 5 chicken breast fillets
- 10 large fresh basil leaves
- 50 g camembert, cut into 5 even pieces
- 400 g (14 oz) can diced tomatoes
- Rice and vegetables or salad, to serve

1. Lay the fillets on a cutting board and carefully cut a pocket opening in the top of each one. Stuff the pocket with 2 basil leaves and a piece of camembert. Close the pockets and secure with toothpicks.
2. Pour the tomatoes into the slow cooker and gently lay each breast in the tomato.
3. Cook on HIGH for 2½ hours or until cooked through.
4. Remove the toothpicks from each breast. Serve topped with the tomato.

Simon Christie

Italian Beef Rolls

This is a warming, hearty dish that the slow cooker turns into a child friendly feast. Pieces of cheaper steak are rolled up with a tasty filling and cooked in a tomato sauce. We moved this family favourite from the oven to the slow cooker so that our son, who didn't like chewy meat, could enjoy it. Once cooked, the meat rolls can be shredded with 2 forks to suit the younger children.

Serves 4 adults and 4 kids • Preparation 25 mins
Cook time 6¼ hours • Cooker capacity 5.5 litres

8 small beef steaks
1 cup chopped parsley
⅓ cup grated parmesan cheese
1 teaspoon garlic paste
8 slices prosciutto
4 carrots, 1 finely diced, 3 cut into 2.5 cm (1 inch) pieces
2 celery stalks, finely diced
1 onion, finely diced
3 potatoes, cut into 4 cm (1¾ inch) chunks
400 g (14 oz) can diced tomatoes
1 cup beef stock
700 g (1 lb 9 oz) bottle passata (puréed tomato)
Steamed rice and vegetables, to serve

1. Use a meat mallet or rolling pin to beat out the steaks so that they are evenly thin.
2. Combine the parsley, parmesan and garlic in a bowl and season with salt and pepper.
3. Place a slice of prosciutto on each steak then press 2 tablespoons of the parsley mixture onto the prosciutto. Roll up each steak and secure with toothpicks. If you like, brown the rolls in a little oil in a frying pan.
4. Place the finely diced vegetables over the base of the slow cooker. Arrange beef rolls in a single layer on top. Add the remaining vegetables, canned tomatoes, stock and passata.
5. Cover and cook on LOW for 6 hours.
6. Serve on a bed of rice with steamed vegetables.

NOTE: Add wine or chopped chilli to the sauce mixture to suit more developed tastes. Instead of rice, try couscous, which nicely absorbs the sauce. Any leftover sauce makes a terrific pasta sauce the next day.

Andrew Millis

SWEET TREATS

Chocolate Rice Pudding

My daughter has a sweet tooth and she loves this!

Serves 4–6 • Preparation 5 mins • Cook 3 hours • Cooker capacity 3.5 litres

180 g (6 oz) short grain rice
6¾ cups chocolate milk
4 tablespoons sugar
1 teaspoon butter
1 teaspoon vanilla extract

1. Place all the ingredients into the slow cooker and stir to combine.
2. Cover and cook on HIGH for 3 hours, stirring every 15–20 minutes.

Rhianna Pittaway

Raspberry & White Chocolate Pudding

There is nothing better in cold weather than a yummy pudding! As my oven had died I decided to adapt this luscious pudding recipe to a slow cooker version. Combining raspberries and bursts of white chocolate with a simple jam sponge roll, it is a delicious treat. As an alternative, use chocolate sponge rolls and strawberries or swap the white chocolate for milk chocolate. If desired, serve with ice cream or a dollop of cream.

Serves 6 • Preparation 10 mins • Cook 3 hours • Cooker capacity 1.5 litres

400 g jam roll, sliced into 14–16 even pieces
2 cups milk
300 ml (10 fl oz) thickened cream
4 eggs, lightly whisked
2 tablespoons caster sugar
200 g (7 oz) white chocolate, chopped
1½ cups frozen raspberries

1. Lightly grease the slow cooker bowl. Arrange half the jam roll slices on base of bowl. Combine the milk, cream, eggs and sugar in a jug and mix well. Pour half the mixture over the jam roll slices.
2. Sprinkle with the chocolate and 1 cup of the raspberries. Top with remaining jam roll slices. Pour over the remaining milk mixture and sprinkle with the remaining raspberries.
3. Cover, putting a tea towel (dish towel) under the lid, and cook on HIGH for 3 hours or until custard is set in the centre.
4. Remove lid and stand for at least 10 minutes before serving.

NOTE: When this rises and sets it just fits in the 1.5 litre bowl. My tea towel was slightly stained by the raspberries on top. You may like to try a 3 litre slow cooker. A plain jam roll is used in this recipe, NOT the roll with cream.

Kerrie Beers

Banana-Berry Loaf

My children love strawberries and bananas, so they wanted to include them in a cake they could enjoy eating and also help to cook. This moist banana-berry cake is perfect by the slice, spread with butter, or warmed up and served with ice cream as a fruity dessert. My 11 year old son helped to create and cook this cake, so it's easy enough for your children to be involved in helping you cook too if you like.

Makes 1 loaf • Preparation 15 mins • Cook 1 hour 20 minutes • Cooker capacity 7 litres

2 cups self-raising flour (wholemeal or white)
⅓ cup sugar
2 eggs, lightly beaten
⅓ cup vegetable oil
½ teaspoon ground cinnamon
250 g (9 oz) strawberries, washed and hulled
1 large ripe banana, sliced

1. Spray a silicon loaf pan lightly with oil or line it with baking paper if you prefer. Pour enough water into the slow cooker bowl so it is 2 cm (¾ inch) deep.
2. Combine the flour, sugar, eggs, oil and cinnamon in a large mixing bowl and mix well.
3. Using a stick blender or food processor, blend strawberries and sliced banana until smooth. Add to the flour mixture and combine well. Pour the mixture into the loaf pan.
4. Cover, putting a tea towel (dish towel) under the lid, and cook on HIGH for 1 hour 20 minutes. Test with a skewer; if it comes out of the cake clean it is cooked. Cookers vary and the loaf may appear moist on top but be cooked inside.
5. Lift out and cool in the pan for 10 minutes, then turn out onto a wire rack. Serve warm or at room temperature.

Caleb, Talyn and Ella Christie

Gingerbread Fudge

I absolutely love homemade gingerbread, but baking it and decorating it can be a hassle and very messy, so I wondered if I could turn the flavours of gingerbread dough into a tasty fudge. I think gingerbread fudge will be a good addition to the pre-Christmas and Christmas feasts with friends and family, but could also be enjoyed during winter for a little spicy warm up. Want more zing? Add more ginger! Want it a bit sweeter? Add more cinnamon!

Makes 24 pieces • Preparation 10 mins • Cook 1 hour • Cooker capacity 5 litres

600 g white chocolate, chopped
395 g (14 oz) can condensed milk
1 tablespoon butter
1 tablespoon brown sugar
2–3 teaspoons ground ginger
1 teaspoon ground nutmeg
1 teaspoon ground cinnamon

1. Combine all the ingredients in the slow cooker.
2. Cook on LOW with the lid off for 50–60 minutes, stirring regularly (my cooker does fudge quickly so you might need longer). Taste after everything has mixed together nicely and adjust spices to your liking. Once the fudge is set on top it's ready.
3. Pour into a lined tray or silicone moulds. Refrigerate overnight, then cut into desired pieces.

NOTE: I sprinkled some home-made gingerbread on top. I like my gingerbread to bite back so I added 1 tablespoon of ginger, but I feel most people would like less.

Cheryl Lordan

Chocolate Caramel Nut Slice

This recipe was the result of a mid-afternoon craving of the sweet variety! Crunchy, chewy, chocolatey and delicious! I absolutely love the combination of chocolate, caramel and peanuts. Add to that the crunchiness and chewiness of chocolate puffed rice cereal (or plain puffed rice if you prefer) and you have an easy, tasty slice for sweet tooths of all ages.

Makes about 20 pieces • Preparation 5 mins • Cook 45 mins • Cooker capacity 3 litres

Spray oil
200 g (7 oz) plain milk chocolate, broken into pieces
100 g (3½ oz) caramel-filled milk chocolate, broken into pieces
2½ tablespoons soft butter
1½ tablespoons crunchy peanut butter
3 snack sized Mars Bars, chopped
6 snack sized Picnic bars, chopped
½ cup salted peanuts
3 cups chocolate puffed rice cereal

1. Spray a 28 x 18 cm (11 x 7 inch) slice pan with oil and line with baking paper. Turn the slow cooker on to HIGH.
2. Place the milk chocolate, caramel-filled chocolate and butter into the slow cooker.
3. Cook uncovered on HIGH for 20–30 minutes. Once nearly all melted add the peanut butter and chopped Mars and Picnic bars. Stir briefly and leave for about 10 minutes, until soft but not completely melted.
4. Stir in the peanuts and chocolate puffed rice, then transfer to the slice pan and press firmly with the back of a spoon. Place in the fridge to set for approximately 2 hours. Once set, remove from tray and cut into squares.

Sharon King

Banana Choc Chunk Muffins

I often can't keep the fruit up to my little fruit bat children (as I call them), but invariably we end up with a few over-ripe bananas here and there. This recipe is perfect to use them up and avoid waste!

Makes 12 • Preparation 15 mins • Cook 1 hour • Cooker capacity 7 litres

- 1½ cups wholemeal (or white) self-raising flour
- ½ cup caster (superfine) sugar
- 3 ripe bananas, mashed
- ⅓ cup milk
- 1 egg
- 1 tablespoon honey
- 100 g (3½ oz) milk chocolate chips

1. Combine the flour and sugar in a mixing bowl. Mix the banana, milk, egg and honey together, then stir into the dry ingredients. Fold the choc chips through.
2. Divide between 12 silicone cupcake cases and place directly on base of a metallic bowl slow cooker. If your slow cooker bowl is ceramic, add about 1 cm water first then sit cases carefully in the shallow water to avoid cooking with a dry cooker.
4. Cover, putting a tea towel (dish towel) under the lid, and cook on HIGH for 1 hour.

NOTE: If you have paper cupcake cases you could elevate them on a trivet above the base or the water.

Paulene Christie

Clinker, Red Frog & Marshmallow Fudge (Kaylah's Fudge)

My 9 year old daughter helped create this recipe with me for a family Christmas party. It has her top three favourite treats in a fudge – who could ask for more?

Makes about 48 pieces • Preparation 5 mins • Cook 45–60 mins • Cooker capacity 3 litres

- 600 g (1 lb 5 oz) milk choc melts
- 395 g (14 oz) can sweetened condensed milk
- 300 g (10½ oz) Pascalls Clinkers
- 190 g (6½ oz) Allens red frogs, cut into quarters
- 100 g (3½ oz) mini marshmallows

1. Place the choc melts and sweetened condensed milk into the slow cooker.
2. Cook, uncovered, on HIGH for 45 minutes to 1 hour, stirring every 10 to 15 minutes, until chocolate has melted and mixture has come together.
3. Turn the slow cooker to LOW. Add the Clinkers, chopped frogs and marshmallows to the mixture and stir to combine. Pour into a 33 x 23 cm (13 x 9 inch) slice pan lined with baking paper. Chill for at least 2 to 3 hours in the fridge, then cut into pieces to serve.

NOTE: If you prefer the frogs and marshmallows to melt into the fudge mixture, add to the slow cooker as soon as the chocolate has melted.

Jodie Leemhuis

Golden Syrup Steamed Mug Puddings

This is a great way to please everyone's taste and preference. Each serve can be different!

Serves 4 • Preparation time 10 mins • Cook 2–2½ hours • Cooker capacity 6 litres

60 g (2 oz) butter
1 cup self-raising flour
2 tablespoons sugar
1 egg
1 cup milk (almost)
Sultanas, optional
⅓–⅔ cup golden syrup

1. Rub the butter and flour together until they resemble breadcrumbs, then stir in the sugar.
2. Crack the egg into a 1 cup measuring jug and fill with milk. Add to the dry ingredients and mix until combined. Add some sultanas to the batter if desired.
3. Lightly grease 4 coffee mugs. Spoon 1–2 tablespoons of golden syrup into the bottom of each mug. Divide the batter between the mugs, and cover each mug with foil.
4. Cover the bottom of the slow cooker with 1cm boiling water then place the mugs in the slow cooker. Cover and cook on HIGH for 2–2½ hours or until cooked.

NOTE: Instead of golden syrup and sultanas, try combinations such as raspberry jam with white choc chips, salted caramel sauce with dark choc chips, or apricot jam with sultanas.

Narelle Youngs

Chocolate Brownies

This recipe is a firm family favourite as voted by my kids! Chocolate-y and fudge-y, it uses the most basic pantry ingredients and is so easy to prepare. We have successfully made this for dessert (served warm with vanilla ice-cream), morning tea, afternoon tea and school fundraiser bake sales. It is a delicious treat in the school lunchbox and freezes well too.

Makes 15 pieces • Preparation 10 mins • Cook 1¼–1½ hours • Cooker capacity 7 litres

¾ cup plain (all-purpose) flour
¼ cup cocoa powder
1 teaspoon baking powder
1 cup sugar
¼–½ cup dark chocolate chips (depending on taste)
2 eggs
1 teaspoon vanilla essence
100 g (3½ oz) butter, melted

1. Line a brownie pan with baking paper extending over the two long sides (check that it will fit into your slow cooker first). Alternatively, line the slow cooker insert with non-stick baking paper if using a smaller slow cooker (see note).
2. Sift the flour, cocoa powder and baking powder into a large mixing bowl. Stir in the sugar and dark chocolate chips and make a well in the centre.
3. Use a fork to whisk the eggs and vanilla together. Add to the flour mixture along with the butter. Stir evenly until combined.
4. Spoon into the prepared brownie pan and place in slow cooker, or spoon into the slow cooker.
5. Cover, putting a tea towel (dish towel) under the lid, and cook on HIGH for about 1¼–1½ hours (it will depend on your slow cooker), until a toothpick inserted comes out clean.
6. Remove pan from slow cooker and stand for 10 minutes. Lift out brownie and place onto a wire rack to cool. Cut into pieces to serve.

NOTE: We usually make this recipe in a brownie pan in a rectangular 7 litre slow cooker. If cooking directly in the slow cooker insert I suggest using a small slow cooker or doubling the recipe.

Esther Hutchings

Strawberry & Apple Crumble

I created this recipe using fresh, in-season fruit and basic pantry ingredients. It has simple steps which kids can easily get involved with, and hopefully they can enjoy the finished product. This is an easy, cheap and relatively healthy dessert. It is great served in cold weather with a scoop of vanilla ice cream. You could substitute raspberries or other berries of your choice for the strawberries.

Serves 2 • Preparation 10 mins • Cook 3 hours • Cooker capacity 1.5 litres

250 g (9 oz) strawberries, halved
1 apple, peeled, cored and diced
½ cup rolled oats
⅓ cup plain (all-purpose) flour
¼ cup brown sugar
2 tablespoons butter, chopped

1. Place the strawberries and apple into the slow cooker.
2. Cover and cook on HIGH for 1 hour.
3. Combine the oats, flour, sugar and butter, rubbing with your fingertips. Sprinkle the crumble topping over the fruit.
4. Cover, putting a tea towel (dish towel) under the lid, and cook on LOW for 2 hours.

Lauren Rimon

Caramel Drops

When I was a child my Aunty Muriel used to make the most delicious jam drop biscuits. I would love helping her to dab the jam in each one and it was with that I mind that I decided to create a new version to make together with my own children. I always have slow cooked caramel on hand, but if you don't and don't want to make some, you can buy ready-made caramel in a can at your supermarket to use for these amazingly more-ish cookies!

Makes 12 • Preparation 20 mins • Cook 1 hour • Cooker capacity 7 litres

- 1½ cups plain (all-purpose) flour
- ⅓ cup caster sugar
- 125 g (4½ oz) butter, softened
- ¼ can slow cooked caramel (see note)

1. Mix the flour and sugar together in a bowl. Add the butter and, using clean hands, thoroughly combine the ingredients to form a crumbly consistency. Roll mixture into 12 small balls (ping pong ball size).
2. Make an indentation in each ball with one of your knuckles. Fill indentation with ½ teaspoon caramel.
3. Line your slow cooker with baking paper. Arrange the cookies over the paper in a single layer.
4. Cover, putting a tea towel (dish towel) under the lid, and cook on HIGH for 1 hour. Carefully lift out and cool on a wire rack.

NOTE: Go to www.slowcookercentral.com/recipe/condensed-milk-caramel/ for instructions on making slow cooked caramel. The cookies are a little soft when first cooked but quickly firm up once cooled.

Paulene Christie

St Clement's Self-saucing Pudding

I hadn't made a self-saucing pudding before but had seen some on the Slow Cooker Central website. I love oranges and lemons, so thought I'd try and include them to make this extremely moreish pudding. I made this for my family and they loved it. Served warm with ice cream, it is sweet and tangy. It certainly was a hit!

Serves 5–6 • Preparation 15 mins • Cook 2 hours • Cooker capacity 1.5 litres

SPONGE
200 g (7 oz) light brown sugar
200 g (7 oz) butter, softened
3 eggs
200 g (7 oz) self-raising flour
Finely grated zest of 3 lemons
Juice of one lemon

SAUCE
100 g (3½ oz) light brown sugar
100 g (3½ oz) golden syrup
Juice of 2 lemons, topped up to 300 ml (10 fl oz) with orange juice

1. Lightly grease the slow cooker bowl. For the sponge, use electric beaters to beat the butter and sugar until creamy. Add the eggs one at a time, beating well after each addition. Fold in the flour, then zest and juice. Place the mixture into the slow cooker bowl.
2. To make the sauce, put the ingredients in a microwavable jug and heat for 90 seconds. Stir to combine and dissolve the sugar. Pour over the sponge batter.
3. Cover, putting a tea towel (dish towel) under the lid, and cook on HIGH for 2 hours.

Joanne Pinnock

PROJECTS

PROJECTS

Yarn Dyeing

These instructions are for single and multi-colour yarn dyeing. Fun for the kids to experiment and see what they come up with!

Preparation 30–60 minutes • Cook 4 hours
• Cooker capacity 3 litres minimum for single colour, 5.5 litres minimum for multi-colour

White or natural-coloured yarn (see note)
Scrap yarn that will not take up the dye (such as 100% acrylic)
White vinegar
Synthetic food colouring (natural food colours do not work)

1. If your yarn isn't already in a hank, then turn it into one. For a smaller quantity of yarn, wind it round the back of a kitchen chair. For a larger quantity, use 2 chairs, being careful not to tighten as you wind thus pulling the chairs together. Tie the scrap yarn loosely round the hank in 4 different places.

2. Place the hank into a large bowl of warm water and white vinegar (¼ cup vinegar to 1 litre water). Make sure there is enough to cover the yarn. Leave to soak for at least 30 minutes.

3. For single colour dyeing, combine 1 litre warm water and the quantity of dye you wish to use (the more dye you use the stronger the colour will be). Place the soaked yarn into the slow cooker, letting it fall naturally into place. If yarn isn't covered with water, add more water until it is. For the single colour dye I used 25 g (¾ oz) of pure wool and 1 tablespoon of colour in 1 litre of water.

4. Cover and cook for 1 hour on HIGH (unless your slow cooker cooks hot) then for 3 hours on LOW. The water should not boil. Some processes talk about the yarn exhausting the dye, meaning that the water will become clear when the process is finished. If you use a larger quantity of dye this may not happen.

5. Remove the yarn from the slow cooker and place into a colander (I use the colander part of my salad spinner). Leave to cool for 15 minutes.

6. After 15 minutes feel how warm the yarn is and run your tap water to that temperature. Rinse yarn until the water is clear – this can take about 10 minutes. It is important that the water isn't too cold or too hot as this can felt your yarn. Place into a salad spinner and spin out the excess water, stopping to drain as you go if necessary. If you don't have a salad spinner then gently squeeze the water out of the yarn and then roll in an old towel to absorb as much water as possible.

7. Once the yarn has as much water as possible removed, hang it up to dry in a warm, dry place. This can take up to 24 hours, depending on the temperature and humidity.

8. For multi-colour dyeing. place the soaked yarn into the slow cooker and cover with warm water. Measure out your dye colours and carefully place them into the water in different areas, and don't agitate at all, to avoid spreading and mixing the colour. I used ½ teaspoon of each colour to dye 50 g (1¾ oz) of yarn in 2 litres of water. The more dye you use, the more likely it is to bleed into the other colours and lose the multi-colour effect.
9. Do not touch the yarn while it is in the water cooking when you are multi-colour dyeing as you will stir it up and mix the colours together which is what you do not want.
10. Cover and cook for 2–4 hours on LOW. The water is not to boil. Use your judgement on whether you think the yarn has finished dyeing. Most of the dye will have been absorbed into the yarn and there should only be a small residual colouration to the water. The yarn I used took 2 hours to dye.
11. Finish the process as in steps 5, 6 and 7. The yarn is now ready for use. Note that it may still lose a little colour when washed so wash separately from other items.

NOTE: The yarn must be a protein-based fibre which comes from an animal, such as wool, alpaca or silk. It could also be a blend of up to 50% acrylic or manmade fibre. Plant-based fibre such as cotton or bamboo doesn't work with this method.

Nikki Willis

Slow Cooker Finger Paints (Non-toxic)

We are always trying to occupy the minds of our little ones, and what better way than to let their imagination run wild with these groovy paints? These are perfectly safe for the children, our homes and our environment. So, what are you waiting for?

Makes about 500 ml (17 fl oz/2 cups) • Preparation 5 mins • Cook 30–45 mins
Cooker capacity 1.5 litres

⅔ cup cornflour (cornstarch)
3 tablespoons caster (superfine) sugar
½ teaspoon salt
Liquid food colouring – red, yellow, blue, green

1. In a bowl, combine the cornflour, caster sugar, salt and 2 cups water. Pour into a slow cooker.
2. Cover, putting a tea towel (dish towel) under the lid, and cook on HIGH for about 30 minutes, or until thickened, stirring occasionally.
3. When the mixture reaches a paint consistency, spoon into storage bottles (baby food jars are great). Add 6 drops of food colouring to each jar, except for red, which needs 25 drops to achieve a rich colour. Screw the lids on tightly and shake each bottle vigorously to mix the colour through the paint.
4. Store, sealed, in the fridge. If the paint gets too thick over time, just add a dash of water and shake vigorously to disperse.

NOTE: You can create additional colours by combining different food colours in each jar. Add glitter for extra sparkle!

Simon Christie

Slow Cooker Play Dough

The texture of this play dough is incomparable to any other. It is silky smooth and non-greasy, and is sure to be a hit with children of all ages.

Makes 1 kg (2 lb 3 oz) • Preparation 10 mins • Cook 45–60 mins • Cooker capacity 5 litres

- 2 cups plain (all-purpose) flour
- ½ cup salt
- ⅓ cup cream of tartar
- 2 tablespoons vegetable oil
- 1–2 teaspoons liquid food colouring

1. In a bowl, combine the flour, salt and cream of tartar. In a separate bowl, combine the oil and 2 cups water.
2. Put the dry ingredients into a slow cooker, add the wet ingredients and mix to combine.
3. Cover, putting a tea towel (dish towel) under the lid, and cook on HIGH for 45–60 minutes, stirring often for the first 30 minutes of cooking time, and then once or twice for the remaining cooking time.
4. The dough is ready when it no longer sticks to the sides of the slow cooker. You can test this by rolling a small amount of dough into a ball and placing it in the freezer for a few minutes. If the dough doesn't stick to your fingers when you remove it from the freezer, it is ready.
5. Remove the dough from the slow cooker, knead until smooth and set aside in an airtight container in the fridge to cool.
6. Divide the play dough into four equal pieces and add food colouring a few drops at a time to each piece, kneading thoroughly to mix. Keep adding and kneading until the play dough is the colour you want.
7. Store the play dough in the fridge.

NOTE: You can add glitter for sparkle, if desired.

Simon Christie

Slime!

Ooey, gooey, green slime! Unlike many home-made slime recipes, this one is non-toxic and fun for children of all ages to play with. We purchased a big bag of psyllium husks for approximately $6 so you can make buckets full of slime for next to nothing! You will find it in the health food aisle of the supermarket.

Makes 1 cup • Preparation 5 mins • Cook 1½ hours • Cooker capacity 1.5 litres

2 tablespoons psyllium husks
A few drops of food colouring of your choice

1. Combine the psyllium husks and 1 cup cold water in the slow cooker. Stir in food colouring, then stir in 1 cup hot tap water.
2. Cook, uncovered, on HIGH for 1½ hours, stirring occasionally.
3. When the slime is ready it will be congealed and stretchy. Let cool before playing!

NOTE: Keep the slime in a sealed container in the fridge. Check before each use that it has no mould, and discard if it does. This was cooked in a 1.5 L slow cooker. A larger one would cook hotter and therefore faster so would need the cooking time reduced.

Simon Christie

INDEX

A

absorbent pads, cooking of 17–18
apples
    Babies' Blue Brekky 37
    Babies' Savoury Veggies with Couscous 35
    Baby Food – Apple with Cinnamon 36
    Kids' Curry 121
    Pork Fillet with Apple and Honey 185
    Pureed Veg for 6+ months 33
    Strawberry & Apple Crumble 258
    Tasty Meatloaf with Apple & Leek by Saz 206
auto function of slow cookers 13
avocados
    Chicken, avocado and broccoli 34

B

baby and toddler foods
    Babies' Blue Brekky 37
    Babies' Savoury Veggies with Couscous 35
    Baby Food – Apple with Cinnamon 36
    Chicken, avocado and broccoli 34
    Pureed Veg for 6+ months 33
bacon
    BBQ Bacon Burgers 223
    Beef and Beans Goulash 191
    Best Baked Beans in the Universe 127
    Breakfast Casserole 43
    Caramelised Onion BBQ Ribs 242
    Caz's Chicken Base Pizza 240
    Caz's Mince Bowls 211
    Cheese & Bacon Croissants 105
    Cheesy Mushroom, Bacon & Onion Eggy Breakfast Slice 45
    Cheesy One Pot Sausage & Veggie Pasta 175
    Chicken with Asparagus and Bacon 179
    Chicken with Camembert Sauce 243
    Cob-less Hot Cob Dip 215
    Creamy Chicken and Chorizo Pasta 181

    Creamy Chicken Delight 86
    Family-friendly Loaded Mince 208
    Hearty Beef & Pasta Stew 172
    Nanna's Chicken Casserole 159
    Tortellini in Tomato Basil Sauce 169
baked beans
    BBQ Bacon Burgers 223
    Beef and Beans Goulash 191
    Best Baked Beans in the Universe 127
    Cheesy Baked Bean Pasties 102
    Easy Cheesy Breakfast Beans 46
    Sticky Vegetarian Sausages 171
    Sweet Chilli Sausages and Beans 95
    See also beans
bananas
    Babies' Blue Brekky 37
    Banana-Berry Loaf 251
    Banana Choc Chunk Muffins 254
bars, *see* slices
beans
    Best Baked Beans in the Universe 127
    Black Bean Quesadillas 237
    Chicken Fiesta 90
    Curried Sausages 183
    Easy Mixed Beans 41
    Shredded Beef Chilli Con Carne 157
    Steph's Beenie Weenies 76
    Sweet Chilli Sausages and Beans 95
    See also baked beans; *see also* refried beans
beef
    BBQ Bacon Burgers 223
    Beef and Beans Goulash 191
    Beef Stew 150
    Caramelised Onion BBQ Ribs 242
    Caz's Mince Bowls 211
    Cheesy Chilli Dogs 220
    Chop Suey 232
    Citrus Silverside & Vegetables 190
    Cola Silverside Surprise 194
    Corned Silverside 130
    Creamy Mushroom Meatballs 201

Dad's Beef Curry 82
Easy Chow Mein 198
Family Friendly Beef Curry 85
Family-friendly Loaded Mince 208
Hearty Beef & Pasta Stew 172
Hidden Veg Lasagne 79
Italian Beef Rolls 245
Kath's Beef Stew 156
Kids' Curry 121
Meatballs in Tomato Sauce 204
Mexican Baguette 104
Nanny's Braised Steak 231
Pizza Sloppy Joes 212
Rich Gravy Mince 197
Rissoles in BBQ sauce 210
Roast Beef with Rich Gravy 160
Shredded Beef Chilli Con Carne 157
Simple Sensational Pulled Beef 118
Simple Taco Mince 111
Spaghetti & Meatballs 202
Sticky Steakhouse Ribs 167
Stroganoff 168
Sweet Orange Silverside 229
Tasty Meatloaf with Apple & Leek by Saz 206
Tasty Tomato Beef in Gravy 113
biscuits
   Caramel Drops 259
   Wagon Wheel Cups 71
blueberries
   Babies' Blue Brekky 37
bok choy, *see* buk choy
breads, rolls & scrolls
   BBQ Bacon Burgers 223
   Cheese & Bacon Croissants 105
   Cheese Rolls 101
   Cheesy Chilli Dogs 220
   Coloured Bread 73
   Easy Peasy Cheesy Rolls 107
   Easymite scrolls 75
   Mexican Baguette 104
   Mexican Pulled Pork Sliders 219
   Pizza Sloppy Joes 212
   Puff Pastry Ham & Cheese Scrolls 74
   Sweet Apple Sultana Damper 100
   Wagon Wheels 72

'bread trick' 12
brie
   Cauliflower Cheese 59
   Chicken with Camembert Sauce 243
broccoli & broccolini
   Babies' Savoury Veggies with Couscous 35
   Chicken, avocado and broccoli 34
   Hearty Beef & Pasta Stew 172
   Pureed Veg for 6+ months 33
   Slow Cooked Shredded Asian Vegetables 141
   3-Ingredient Alfredo Chicken and Broccoli 193
brownies 257
browning meat when slow cooking 15–16
buk choy
   Asian Greens 61
burgers
   BBQ Bacon Burgers 223

C

cabbage
   Chop Suey 232
   Easy Chow Mein 198
   Slow Cooked Shredded Asian Vegetables 141
cakes
   Banana-Berry Loaf 251
   Banana Choc Chunk Muffins 254
   Chocolate Brownies 257
   Coconut Cake 217
   Sweet Apple Sultana Damper 100
   techniques for slow cooking cakes 24–5
camembert
   Camembert and Basil Breast Pockets 244
   Chicken with Camembert Sauce 243
capsicum
   Beef and Beans Goulash 191
   Caz's Chicken Base Pizza 240
   Caz's Easy Peasy Kebabs 216
   Caz's Mince Bowls 211
   Chicken Fiesta 90
   Chicken Fried Rice 125
   Chop Suey 232

Herbed Chicken 166
Kids' Curry 121
Pizza Sloppy Joes 212
Sausage Bolognese 126
Shredded Beef Chilli Con Carne 157
Spanish Chicken 230
Sweet Chilli Cashew Chicken 139
Sweet & Sour Pork Rashers 188
caramel
   Caramel Drops 259
   Chocolate Caramel Nut Slice 253
carrots
   Babies' Savoury Veggies with Couscous 35
   Beef Stew 150
   Butter Chicken Meatballs 205
   Cheat's Italian Meatballs (With Hidden Veg) 207
   Chicken Fried Rice 125
   Chicken Soup 151
   Chop Suey 232
   Citrus-infused Silverside 229
   Creamy Country Chicken Casserole 155
   Creamy Vegetable Curry 112
   Curried Sausages 183
   Dad's Beef Curry 82
   Easy Chow Mein 198
   Hearty Beef & Pasta Stew 172
   Hidden Veg Lasagne 79
   Italian Beef Rolls 245
   Kath's Beef Stew 156
   Kids' Curry 121
   Pureed Veg for 6+ months 33
   Slow Cooked Duck and Veggies 233
   Slow Cooked Saucy Shanks 154
   Slow Cooked Shredded Asian Vegetables 141
   Spaghetti & Meatballs 202
   Sweet Chilli Cashew Chicken 139
cashews
   Sweet Chilli Cashew Chicken 139
casseroles & stews
   Beef and Beans Goulash 191
   Beef Stew 150
   Breakfast Casserole 43
   Chicken Cordon Bleu Casserole 235

   Creamy Country Chicken Casserole 155
   Hearty Beef & Pasta Stew 172
   Hungarian Chicken 227
   Kath's Beef Stew 156
   Nanna's Chicken Casserole 159
   Nanny's Braised Steak 231
   Old Favourite Casserole Chops 147
   Sausage Ragout 80
   Slow Cooked Saucy Shanks 154
   Taco Mushroom Sausages 153
   Tasty Tomato Beef in Gravy 113
   See also curries
cauliflower
   Cauliflower Cheese 59
   Creamy Cauliflower and Prosciutto Soup 234
   Creamy Vegetable Curry 112
celery
   Chicken Fried Rice 125
   Chicken Soup 151
   Chop Suey 232
   Dad's Beef Curry 82
   Easy Chow Mein 198
   Italian Beef Rolls 245
   Kath's Beef Stew 156
cheese
   Black Bean Quesadillas 237
   Breakfast Casserole 43
   Camembert and Basil Breast Pockets 244
   Cauliflower Cheese 59
   Caz's 3 Cs Dish 94
   Caz's Chicken Base Pizza 240
   Caz's Fish Finger Brekky Bake 44
   Caz's Mince Bowls 211
   Cheese & Bacon Croissants 105
   Cheesy Baked Bean Pasties 102
   Cheesy Chicken One Pot Pasta 165
   Cheesy Mushroom, Bacon & Onion Eggy Breakfast Slice 45
   Cheesy One Pot Sausage & Veggie Pasta 175
   Cheesy Potato Soup 152
   Chicken Cordon Bleu Casserole 235
   Chicken with Camembert Sauce 243
   Cob-less Hot Cob Dip 215

Creamy Cheesy Chicken and Pasta 84
Creamy Garlic Chicken Made Easy 120
Easy Cheesy Breakfast Beans 46
Easymite scrolls 75
Easy Peasy Cheesy Rolls 107
4 Ingredient Potato Bake 52
Hidden Veg Lasagne 79
Italian Beef Rolls 245
Mexican Baguette 104
Morning Mushrooms 42
Naked Chicken Parmigiana 114
One Pot Chicken Alfredo Pasta 186
Puff Pastry Ham & Cheese Scrolls 74
Ratatouille 239
Savoury Cheese Spread 101
Slow Cooked Pizza 140
Sweet BBQ Pulled Pork Nachos 144
Tuna, Mac & Cheese 96

chicken
  Barbecue Chicken Drumsticks 88
  Big Mac Chicken 83
  Butter Chicken Meatballs 205
  Camembert and Basil Breast Pockets 244
  Carbonara Chicken Meatballs 200
  Caz's Chicken Base Pizza 240
  Caz's Easy Peasy Kebabs 216
  Cheesy Chicken One Pot Pasta 165
  Chicken and Gravy 116
  Chicken, avocado and broccoli 34
  Chicken, Chorizo and Vegetable One-Pot Dinner 87
  Chicken Cordon Bleu Casserole 235
  Chicken Fiesta 90
  Chicken Fried Rice 125
  Chicken Potato Pie 149
  Chicken Soup 151
  Chicken with Asparagus and Bacon 179
  Chicken with Camembert Sauce 243
  Chilli Kicker Chicken 97
  Creamy Cheesy Chicken and Pasta 84
  Creamy Chicken and Chorizo Pasta 181
  Creamy Chicken Cup a Laksa 148
  Creamy Chicken Delight 86
  Creamy Chicken with Herb Gravy 131
  Creamy Country Chicken Casserole 155
  Creamy Garlic Chicken Made Easy 120
  Creamy Mexican Chicken 178
  Crumbed Chicken Nuggets 70
  Easy Budget BBQ Chicken 117
  Easy Chicken & Pasta 89
  Fast 'n' Simple Marinated Wings – 3 Ways 184
  French Cream Chicken 103
  Herbed Chicken 166
  Honey Mustard Chicken Wings 187
  Hungarian Chicken 227
  Loaded Spanish Bake 173
  Mango Chutney Chicken Wings 69
  Mexican Chicken Porcupines 203
  Milo's Creamy Pesto Chicken Meatballs 164
  Naked Chicken Parmigiana 114
  Nanna's Chicken Casserole 159
  One Pot Chicken Alfredo Pasta 186
  Orange BBQ Chicken 137
  Poached Asian Chicken 106
  Roast Chicken – Stuffed Full of Flavour 122
  Satay Chicken & Spinach 182
  Satay Wings 98
  Saucy Chicken 115
  slow cooking whole 16
  Spanish Chicken 230
  Sticky Chicken Wings 65
  Stroganoff 168
  Sweet Chilli Cashew Chicken 139
  Sweet Peanut Satay Chicken Skewers 142
  Sweet Soy Asian Chicken 134
  Texas BBQ Shredded Chicken 170
  3 Ingredient Alfredo Chicken and Broccoli 193
  Tomato Sauce and Brown Sugar Chicken 174

chocolate
  Banana Choc Chunk Muffins 254
  Chocolate Bread and Butter Pudding 93
  Chocolate Brownies 257
  Chocolate Caramel Nut Slice 253
  Chocolate Rice Pudding 249
  Chocolate Spiders 218

Clinker, Red Frog & Marshmallow Fudge 255
Gingerbread Fudge 252
Marshmallow Monsters 222
Mini M&M's LCMs 221
Raspberry & White Chocolate Pudding 250
suitability for fudge 25
Wagon Wheel Cups 71
chorizo
Chicken, Chorizo and Vegetable One-Pot Dinner 87
Loaded Spanish Bake 173
Spanish Chicken 230
cleaning slow cookers 20–2
coconut
Coconut Cake 217
Curried Sausages 183
Family Friendly Beef Curry 85
Slow Cooker Corn 53
Sweet Peanut Satay Chicken Skewers 142
Coco Pops (chocolate puffed rice cereal)
Chocolate Caramel Nut Slice 253
Mini M&M's LCMs 221
converting cooking times for slow cookers 29
converting recipes for slow cooking 28–9
cookies, see biscuits
corn
Black Bean Quesadillas 237
Cheesy Chicken One Pot Pasta 165
Chicken Fiesta 90
Chicken Fried Rice 125
Curried Sausages 183
Family-friendly Loaded Mince 208
Pureed Veg for 6+ months 33
Slow Cooker Corn 53
Sweet Potato & Corn Soup 180
Tuna, Mac & Cheese 96
corn chips
Caz's 3 Cs Dish 94
cornflour as thickener 9–10
couscous
Babies' Savoury Veggies with Couscous 35

crafts & projects
Finger Paints 265
Play Dough 266
Slime 267
Yarn Dyeing 263–4
cream, splitting problems associated with 19–20
croissants
Cheese & Bacon Croissants 105
curries
Creamy Vegetable Curry 112
Curried Sausages 183
Dad's Beef Curry 82
Family Friendly Beef Curry 85

D

dairy products, splitting problems associated with 19–20
desserts, see puddings
diet recipes for slow cookers 22–3
dim sims
Sweet Chilli Dim Sims 143
dips
Cob-less Hot Cob Dip 215
duck
Slow Cooked Duck and Veggies 233
dumplings
Sweet Chilli Dim Sims 143

E

eggs
Breakfast Casserole 43
Caz's Fish Finger Brekky Bake 44
Cheese & Bacon Croissants 105
Cheesy Mushroom, Bacon & Onion Eggy Breakfast Slice 45
Chicken Fried Rice 125
Chocolate Bread and Butter Pudding 93
Easy Chow Mein 198
Egg and Mayo Pasties 67
Loaded Spanish Bake 173
Raspberry & White Chocolate Pudding 250
Scrambled Eggs 47

F

fat and oil, removal of from slow cooked food 12–13
feta
   Breakfast Casserole 43
Finger Paints 265
fish fingers
   Caz's Fish Finger Brekky Bake 44
flour as thickener in slow cooking 11
food safety
   absorbent pads, cooking of 17–19
   risks from frozen meat 8
   storage risks 20
   temperature risks 20
   toxicity of kidney beans 24
frankfurts
   Caz's 3 Cs Dish 94
   Easy Cheesy Breakfast Beans 46
   Hot Dogs Put Together 138
   Steph's Beenie Weenies 76
   Sweet Chilli Sausages and Beans 95
   See also sausages
frozen meat, safety of in slow cooking 8–9
fudge
   Clinker, Red Frog & Marshmallow Fudge 255
   Gingerbread Fudge 252
   slow cooking techniques for 25–7

H

ham
   Best Baked Beans in the Universe 127
   Chicken Cordon Bleu Casserole 235
   4 Ingredient Potato Bake 52
   Puff Pastry Ham & Cheese Scrolls 74

K

kabana
   Caz's Easy Peasy Kebabs 216
kebabs & skewers
   Caz's Easy Peasy Kebabs 216
   Garlic Prawn or Chicken Skewers 236
   Sweet Peanut Satay Chicken Skewers 142
kidney beans, toxicity associated with 24

L

lamb
   French Onion Chops 192
   Greek Style Lemon & Herb Lamb Leg 228
   Old Favourite Casserole Chops 147
   Pulled Roast Lamb in Gravy 158
   Roast Leg Lamb with Sweet Chilli Sauce 133
   Slow Cooked Saucy Shanks 154
lasagne
   Hidden Veg Lasagne 79
leeks
   Creamy Country Chicken Casserole 155
   Tasty Meatloaf with Apple & Leek by Saz 206
lemons
   St Clements Self-saucing Pudding 260
low-fat slow cooking 22–3

M

marshmallows
   Clinker, Red Frog & Marshmallow Fudge 255
   Gooey Rice Bubble Bars 99
   Marshmallow Monsters 222
   Mini M&M's LCMs 221
   Wagon Wheel Cups 71
meat, browning when slow cooking 15–16
meatballs
   Butter Chicken Meatballs 205
   Cheat's Italian Meatballs (With Hidden Veg) 207
   Creamy Mushroom Meatballs 201
   Easy Meatballs and Gravy 199
   Meatballs in Tomato Sauce 204
   Mexican Chicken Porcupines 203
   Milo's Creamy Pesto Chicken Meatballs 164
   Spaghetti & Meatballs 202
   Swedish-style Meatballs 163
   Turkey Meatballs 209
meatloaf
   Tasty Meatloaf with Apple & Leek by Saz 206

minestrone
  Lydia's Minestrone Alphabet Soup 81
muffins
  Banana Choc Chunk Muffins 254
mushrooms
  Beef Stew 150
  Cheesy Mushroom, Bacon & Onion Eggy Breakfast Slice 45
  Chicken and Gravy 116
  Chop Suey 232
  Creamy Chicken Delight 86
  Creamy Paprika Pork 238
  Family-friendly Loaded Mince 208
  Herbed Chicken 166
  Hidden Veg Lasagne 79
  Hot Dogs Put Together 138
  Morning Mushrooms 42
  Pizza Sloppy Joes 212
  Sausage Ragout 80
  Spaghetti & Meatballs 202
  Stroganoff 168
  Taco Mushroom Sausages 153

N
nachos
  Sweet BBQ Pulled Pork Nachos 144
noodles
  Chicken Soup 151
  Chocolate Spiders 218
  Easy Chow Mein 198
  See also pasta

O
oats
  Babies' Blue Brekky 37
  Strawberry & Apple Crumble 258
oil and fat, removal of from slow cooked food 12–13
olives
  Spanish Chicken 230
oven to slow cooker conversions 28–9

P
pak choy
  Asian Greens 61
parsley
  Greek Style Lemon & Herb Lamb Leg 228
  Italian Beef Rolls 245
parsnips
  Babies' Savoury Veggies with Couscous 35
  Beef Stew 150
pasta
  Beef and Beans Goulash 191
  Big Mac Chicken 83
  Cheat's Italian Meatballs (With Hidden Veg) 207
  Cheesy Chicken One Pot Pasta 165
  Cheesy One Pot Sausage & Veggie Pasta 175
  Creamy Cheesy Chicken and Pasta 84
  Creamy Chicken and Chorizo Pasta 181
  Creamy Paprika Pork 238
  Easy Chicken & Pasta 89
  Hearty Beef & Pasta Stew 172
  Hidden Veg Lasagne 79
  Lydia's Minestrone Alphabet Soup 81
  Meatballs in Tomato Sauce 204
  Milo's Creamy Pesto Chicken Meatballs 164
  One Pot Chicken Alfredo Pasta 186
  Spaghetti & Meatballs 202
  Sweet Chilli Cashew Chicken 139
  Tortellini in Tomato Basil Sauce 169
  Tuna, Mac & Cheese 96
pastry
  Caz's Easy Peasy Sausage Rolls 66
  Cheesy Baked Bean Pasties 102
  Easymite scrolls 75
  Egg and Mayo Pasties 67
  Puff Pastry Ham & Cheese Scrolls 74
peanut butter
  Chocolate Caramel Nut Slice 253
  Chocolate Spiders 218
  Satay Chicken & Spinach 182
  Satay Wings 98
  Sweet Peanut Satay Chicken Skewers 142
peas
  Cheesy Chicken One Pot Pasta 165
  Chicken Fried Rice 125

Creamy Vegetable Curry 112
    Curried Sausages 183
    Kath's Beef Stew 156
    Milo's Creamy Pesto Chicken Meatballs
        164
    Pureed Veg for 6+ months 33
    Tuna, Mac & Cheese 96
phytohaemagglutinin in kidney beans 24
pineapple
    Caribbean Rice 57
    Caz's Easy Peasy Kebabs 216
    Dad's Beef Curry 82
    Sweet Chilli Cashew Chicken 139
    Sweet & Sour Pork Rashers 188
pizza
    Caz's Chicken Base Pizza 240
    Pizza Sloppy Joes 212
    Slow Cooked Pizza 140
Play Dough 266
pork
    Cantonese Pork Pieces 177
    Creamy Paprika Pork 238
    Easy Meatballs and Gravy 199
    Jodie's Awesome Roast Pork 241
    Mexican Pulled Pork Sliders 219
    Pork and Gravy 128
    Pork Fillet with Apple and Honey 185
    Pulled Pork on Your Fork 119
    Saucy Pork Cutlets 123
    Stroganoff 168
    Swedish-style Meatballs 163
    Sweet BBQ Pulled Pork Nachos 144
    Sweet & Sour Pork Rashers 188
potato as thickener in slow cooking 10
potato gems
    Breakfast Casserole 43
potatoes
    Babies' Savoury Veggies with Couscous
        35
    Baked Baby Potatoes 54
    Caz's Mashed Potato 58
    Cheesy Potato Soup 152
    Chicken, Chorizo and Vegetable One-Pot
        Dinner 87
    Chicken Potato Pie 149
    Citrus-infused Silverside 229

Creamy Country Chicken Casserole
    155
Creamy Potatoes 55
4 Ingredient Potato Bake 52
Hearty Beef & Pasta Stew 172
Honey Mustard Sausage Pot 176
Italian Beef Rolls 245
Kath's Beef Stew 156
Loaded Spanish Bake 173
Pureed Veg for 6+ months 33
Ratatouille 239
Slow Cooked Duck and Veggies 233
Taco Mushroom Sausages 153
Tuna Patties 68
prawns
    Garlic Prawn or Chicken Skewers 236
prosciutto
    Creamy Cauliflower and Prosciutto Soup
        234
    Garlic Prawn or Chicken Skewers 236
    Italian Beef Rolls 245
puddings
    Chocolate Bread and Butter Pudding 93
    Chocolate Rice Pudding 249
    Golden Syrup Steamed Mug Puddings
        256
    Raspberry & White Chocolate Pudding
        250
    St Clements Self-saucing Pudding 260
    Strawberry & Apple Crumble 258
pumpkin
    Babies' Savoury Veggies with Couscous
        35
    Creamy Vegetable Curry 112
    Pureed Veg for 6+ months 33
purees, *see* baby and toddler foods

Q
quesadillas
    Black Bean Quesadillas 237

R
raspberries
    Raspberry & White Chocolate Pudding
        250
Ratatouille 239

Index | 275

refried beans
　Mexican Rice 56
rice
　Babies' Blue Brekky 37
　Black Bean Quesadillas 237
　Brown Rice 51
　Caribbean Rice 57
　Chicken Fried Rice 125
　Chocolate Rice Pudding 249
　Mexican Chicken Porcupines 203
　Mexican Rice 56
Rice Bubbles (puffed rice cereal)
　Gooey Rice Bubble Bars 99
　Marshmallow Monsters 222
　Mini M&M's LCMs 221
rissoles
　Rissoles in BBQ sauce 210
rolls, see breads, rolls & scrolls

S
safety of slow cookers 14
sauces
　Tomato Sauce 60
sausages
　BBQ Sausages 124
　Breakfast Casserole 43
　Caz's Easy Peasy Kebabs 216
　Caz's Easy Peasy Sausage Rolls 66
　Cheat's Italian Meatballs (With Hidden Veg) 207
　Cheesy One Pot Sausage & Veggie Pasta 175
　Chicken, Chorizo and Vegetable One-Pot Dinner 87
　Creamy Chicken and Chorizo Pasta 181
　Curried Sausages 183
　Easy Tomato Sausages 189
　Honey Mustard Sausage Pot 176
　Loaded Spanish Bake 173
　Milo's Creamy Pesto Chicken Meatballs 164
　Sausage Bolognese 126
　Sausage Ragout 80
　Spanish Chicken 230
　Sticky Vegetarian Sausages 171
　Taco Mushroom Sausages 153
　Tasty Meatloaf with Apple & Leek by Saz 206
　See also frankfurts
scrolls, see breads, rolls & scrolls
silverside
　Citrus-infused Silverside 229
　Citrus Silverside & Vegetables 190
　Cola Silverside Surprise 194
　Corned Silverside 130
skewers & kebabs
　Caz's Easy Peasy Kebabs 216
　Garlic Prawn or Chicken Skewers 236
　Sweet Peanut Satay Chicken Skewers 142
slices
　Chocolate Brownies 257
　Chocolate Caramel Nut Slice 253
　Gooey Rice Bubble Bars 99
　Marshmallow Monsters 222
　Mini M&M's LCMs 221
sliders
　Mexican Pulled Pork Sliders 219
Slime 267
soups
　Cheesy Potato Soup 152
　Chicken Soup 151
　Creamy Cauliflower and Prosciutto Soup 234
　Lydia's Minestrone Alphabet Soup 81
　Sweet Potato & Corn Soup 180
spinach
　Babies' Savoury Veggies with Couscous 35
　Chop Suey 232
　Family-friendly Loaded Mince 208
　French Cream Chicken 103
　Satay Chicken & Spinach 182
　Sticky Vegetarian Sausages 171
　Stroganoff 168
split cream, problems with 19–20
squash
　Chop Suey 232
　Family-friendly Loaded Mince 208
staple foods for slow cooking 28
stews, see casseroles & stews

stovetop to slow cooker conversions 28–9
strawberries
    Banana-Berry Loaf 251
    Strawberry & Apple Crumble 258
sultanas
    Sweet Apple Sultana Damper 100
swedes
    Beef Stew 150
sweet potatoes
    Babies' Savoury Veggies with Couscous 35
    Hot Dogs Put Together 138
    Pureed Veg for 6+ months 33
    Ratatouille 239
    Sweet Potato & Corn Soup 180
sweets
    Caramel Drops 259
    Chocolate Caramel Nut Slice 253
    Chocolate Spiders 218
    Clinker, Red Frog & Marshmallow Fudge 255
    Gingerbread Fudge 252
    Gooey Rice Bubble Bars 99
    Marshmallow Monsters 222
    Mini M&M's LCMs 221
    See also biscuits; *see also* cakes; *see also* puddings; *see also* slices

T

tacos
    Simple Taco Mince 111
'tea towel trick' 10, 11–12
thickening slow cooked dishes 9–10
timers, use of with slow cooking 13–14
times, converting for slow cookers 29
tomatoes
    Best Baked Beans in the Universe 127
    Breakfast Casserole 43
    Butter Chicken Meatballs 205
    Camembert and Basil Breast Pockets 244
    Caribbean Rice 57
    Caz's 3 Cs Dish 94
    Caz's Chicken Base Pizza 240
    Caz's Easy Peasy Kebabs 216
    Caz's Fish Finger Brekky Bake 44
    Cheat's Italian Meatballs (With Hidden Veg) 207
    Cheesy Chilli Dogs 220
    Cheesy One Pot Sausage & Veggie Pasta 175
    Chicken, Chorizo and Vegetable One-Pot Dinner 87
    Curried Sausages 183
    Family-friendly Loaded Mince 208
    Hearty Beef & Pasta Stew 172
    Hot Dogs Put Together 138
    Hungarian Chicken 227
    Italian Beef Rolls 245
    Kath's Beef Stew 156
    Loaded Spanish Bake 173
    Lydia's Minestrone Alphabet Soup 81
    Meatballs in Tomato Sauce 204
    Mexican Chicken Porcupines 203
    Mexican Pulled Pork Sliders 219
    Mexican Rice 56
    Morning Mushrooms 42
    Old Favourite Casserole Chops 147
    Ratatouille 239
    Sausage Ragout 80
    Shredded Beef Chilli Con Carne 157
    Slow Cooked Saucy Shanks 154
    Spaghetti & Meatballs 202
    Spanish Chicken 230
    Sticky Vegetarian Sausages 171
    Tasty Tomato Beef in Gravy 113
    Tomato Sauce 60
tuna
    Tuna, Mac & Cheese 96
    Tuna Patties 68
turkey
    Slow Cooker Turkey 132
    Tasty Turkey Drumsticks 129
    Turkey Meatballs 209

V

veal
    Easy Meatballs and Gravy 199
Vegemite
    Easymite scrolls 75

W
weight loss and slow cooking 22–3
wombok
   Slow Cooked Shredded Asian
      Vegetables 141

Y
Yarn Dyeing 263–4

Z
zucchini
   Butter Chicken Meatballs 205
   Cheat's Italian Meatballs (With Hidden
      Veg) 207
   Chop Suey 232
   Family-friendly Loaded Mince 208
   Hidden Veg Lasagne 79
   Kids' Curry 121
   Ratatouille 239
   Spaghetti & Meatballs 202

THANK YOU

Thank you to the wonderful people who assist me every day to administer our massive Facebook group: Felicity, Karen, Nikki, Denise, Victoria and Simon … you help not only me, but also our half million members every day to make our group the safe, supportive and informative community it is!

Thank you to Brigitta Doyle, Director of ABC Books, and my fairy bookmother :) Your vision for our books and all they could become changed my life forever. Never underestimate the respect and gratitude I have for you and for that fateful day you entered my life and made me an 'author'. x

Thank you to Lachlan McLaine and Matthew Howard and all the team at ABC Books and HarperCollins Australia. This team are with me every step of the way as I navigate the publishing world and are an endless wealth of knowledge, support and encouragement.

For my friends near and far, especially Julie and Kris, who always support me, always encourage me, always care.

For my family, Dad, Vicki and Debbie. Look what the baby of the family did again – book four, can you believe it!?

For Simon, my groom, my soulmate, who has shared the last 25 years of my life and who shall share all my remaining days – nothing and no one supports me in life more than you. You are my rock in any storm, my cheer squad in any challenge, my comfort in any time of need, my everything and my always. x

For our beautiful, spirited, inspiring and enchanting children – you are our world. I love how you proudly tell others about these books. My hope is you will always be proud of me and one day will show your children the books I have written and tell them tales of Mumma and her many slow cookers ;) I love you all more than I can ever put into words. xx

Last but certainly not least, to all of our group members, to all of our website and app members, and most importantly, to each and every one of you who shared your own recipes for these books – THANK YOU! We would not have our community of passionate slow cooking fans without you!

I love the online family we have all created, sharing ideas, sharing support, sharing meals and even sharing the odd mishaps :) You are the reason that slow cooking work is the first thing I do when I open my eyes every day, the last thing I do before I go to bed every night, and what I do throughout every single day of the last five years. I'm so thankful to have each and every one of you a part of this amazing slow cooking family we have created! So THANK YOU. xx

Slow-cooking internet sensation Paulene Christie is a busy working mum with a passion for sharing new and exciting recipes for the slow cooker. She now has more than 515,000 members in her Facebook group, Slow Cooker Recipes 4 Families, and a hugely successful website, Slow Cooker Central. The Facebook page is so popular that Paulene has a team of six people (including her husband, Simon) to help her administer the thousands of recipes and comments that are posted each day. Paulene lives in Queensland with Simon, their three young children and 22 slow cookers.

www.slowcookercentral.com
www.facebook.com/groups/SlowCookerRecipes4Families